Vocabu-Lit
Building Vocabulary Through Literature

Book G

Teacher Guide

Perfection Learning®

Acknowledgments

Excerpt from *Alex Haley: Author of Roots* by Doreen Gonzales. Copyright © 1994 by Doreen Gonzales. Reprinted by permission of Enslow Publishers, Inc.

Excerpt from *Annie John* by Jamaica Kincaid. Copyright © 1985 by Jamaica Kincaid. Reprinted by permission of Farrar, Straus & Giroux, LLC.

Excerpt from *The Red Pony* by John Steinbeck. Copyright 1937, 1938 by John Steinbeck. Reprinted by permission of The Viking Press, a division of Penguin Putnam Inc.

Excerpt from *The Old Man and the Sea* by Ernest Hemingway. Copyright 1952 by Ernest Hemingway; copyright renewed © 1980 by Mary Hemingway. Reprinted by permission of Scribner, a division of Simon & Schuster, Inc.

Excerpt from *¡Yo!* by Julia Alvarez. Copyright © 1997 by Julia Alvarez. Published by Algonquin Books of Chapel Hill. Reprinted by permission of Susan Bergholz Literary Services, New York. All rights reserved.

Excerpt from *Catherine, Called Birdy* by Karen Cushman. Copyright © 1994 by Karen Cushman. Reprinted by permission of Clarion Books/Houghton Mifflin Co. All rights reserved.

Excerpt from *Chapters: My Growth as a Writer* by Lois Duncan. Copyright © 1948, 1960, 1961, 1963, 1967, 1969, 1971, 1982 by Lois Duncan. Reprinted by permission of Little, Brown and Company, Inc.

Perfection Learning®

Text © 2002 © 1991 by Perfection Learning® Corporation.
All rights reserved. No part of this book may be used or reproduced in
any manner whatsoever without written permission from the publisher.
Printed in the United States of America. For information, contact
Perfection Learning® Corporation, 1000 North Second Avenue,
P.O. Box 500, Logan, Iowa 51546-0500.
Tel: 1-800-831-4190 • Fax: 1-800-543-2745
perfectionlearning.com

Paperback ISBN 0-7891-5650-4
7 8 9 10 11 12 PP 10 09 08 07 06 05

Table of Contents

Using the *Vocabu-Lit* Program

Vocabu-Lit is a unique lit-based program designed to help your students improve their word power. In format and approach, it differs in several ways from the usual vocabulary-building materials.

First, *Vocabu-Lit* contains examples of how the vocabulary words have been used by various writers and speakers. The inclusion of classic and high-interest literature not only will interest students in good writing but also will show them how vocabulary can become an effective writing tool.

Second, *Vocabu-Lit* does not ask students to learn a large number of words at one sitting. Instead, students master just ten words at a time and are provided several experiences with those words. Each experience reinforces the previous one, helping students to master meaning.

Third, *Vocabu-Lit* capitalizes on students' natural approach to language acquisition by having them study words in context. Learning words through context aids students in two ways. First, it leads them to define a word more precisely. It also helps them develop an important reading skill: the ability to discover and use contextual clues to determine meaning.

Reading the Passage

Each lesson begins with a selection from a book, essay, story, poem, or speech. Students are encouraged to read straight through the selection without paying particular attention to the Master Words (the ten words in dark type). Their understanding of the general meaning of the passage should help them determine the definitions of the Master Words. Students are advised to read the passage again, this time paying closer attention to the Master Words.

Self-Testing for Understanding

The first exercise is a self-test designed to help students identify the words which they have not yet mastered. Often students will think they know a Master Word only to find that the contextual meaning of the word differs from their own understanding of its meaning. Or they may be unable to state the exact definition. This exercise teaches students to examine a word in context and define its meaning more precisely.

Sometimes the word is actually defined by the context. For example, "He was a *mendicant* because he had to beg." Other times, opposite or contrasting terms reveal the word's meaning: "He was far from poor; in fact he was *affluent.*" Sometimes an unfamiliar word may be followed by examples that explain it, as in "Mrs. Murphy was a *hospitable* woman who warmly welcomed her son's friends." From the context, which in this case consists of an example, the students should have little difficulty figuring out that *hospitable* means "giving a friendly welcome to guests." Selections may also include key words such as *means, is, for example, in other words,* or *and so forth.* All of these are clues which help the students determine a word's meaning.

Note: In some cases, the form of the Master word in the self-test is not the same as in the passage. Generally, these changes were made to provide students with a more commonly used form of the word.

Writing Definitions

In the second exercise, students are asked to write definitions of the Master Words. The first part of the exercise asks that they define as many of the ten words as they can without using a dictionary. Students should use contextual clues and any previous experience with the words to write their definitions.

The second part of the exercise asks that the students consult a dictionary and copy an appropriate definition for each word in the space provided. A reproducible glossary is provided in the back of this teacher's edition should you wish to substitute it for a dictionary.

Note: the part of speech of the words as they will be used in the *exercises* is already indicated in the exercise. This may be different from the words' function in the passage, but students may still find contextual clues helpful.

Choosing Synonyms and Antonyms

In this exercise, students pick a synonym and antonym for each Master Word. Before students begin the lesson, you may wish to review the meanings of *synonym* and *antonym.*

Since students may not be familiar with all

the words in the list of synonyms and antonyms, they may find it useful to keep dictionaries handy.

Note: There are no appropriate antonyms for some Master Words. In such cases, the antonym blank has been marked with an X. Also, a synonym or antonym may sometimes match more than one Master Word in the exercise. Both possible answers are indicated in the teacher edition.

Completing Analogies

In the fourth exercise, students complete word analogies using the Master Words. Again, students will be working with synonyms and antonyms (though different from those in the third exercise).

Before attempting to complete this activity, students should be shown how to read analogies. Try introducing them to the concept with the following example.

day : night :: rich : ________________

Tell students that the symbol **:** means "is to" and **::** means "as." Thus, the analogy could be read "Day is to night as rich is to __________."

Point out to students that the words *day* and *night* are opposites, or antonyms. So they should look for an antonym of *rich* in their list of Master Words. The Master Word *penniless* would be a correct response.

Fitting Words into Context

The next exercise includes ten sentences, which students complete with the appropriate Master Words. Each sentence supplies clues to help students select the best answer. Thus, while testing understanding of the new words, this exercise also provides another contextual setting for the Master Words.

Playing with the Words

In the final exercise, students use the Master Words to solve a variety of puzzles. Traditional games such as acrostic, crosswords, and word spirals are offered. But there are also more novel puzzles that challenge students to arrange words by degree, play associations, complete word fact tables, and invent definitions for portmanteau (or merged) Master Words. They are even invited to write stories using some of their newly acquired vocabulary.

Reviewing Knowledge

There are three review lessons in every *Vocabu-Lit* (Lessons 12, 24, and 36). Students test their mastery of the vocabulary words from the previous eleven lessons by completing sentences and analogies.

Read the following selection to get the general meaning. Read it a second time, paying special attention to the words in dark type. Notice how they are used in sentences. These are Master Words. These are the words you will be working with in this section.

from **Alex Haley: Author of Roots**
by Doreen Gonzales

Roots: The Saga of an American Family, by Alex Haley, hit the bookstores in October, 1976. By January, 1977 it was the best-selling nonfiction book in America. Nearly one-half million copies had already been sold.

Haley, who had moved to Los Angeles when he finished the **manuscript**, spent much of his time traveling around the country **promoting** *Roots*. Wherever he went crowds greeted him.

The book moved many people. In Los Angeles, where over three thousand people lined up for Haley's autograph, an African American woman told him, "This is not a book, this is my history."

And a white Californian wrote to Haley, "You have given me a new **awareness** of your **heritage**. The people of Africa came alive and with them their beauty, pride, tradition, and strength. Kunta Kinte is now part of me. I will carry him, his family, and his country with me and, hopefully, this new awareness will make me a better human being."

Many book reviewers liked *Roots* too. In *Newsweek* magazine, Paul D. Zimmerman said that Haley had written a book that was "bold in **concept**" and would "reach millions of people and **alter** the way we see ourselves."

In the *New York Times Book Review*, Jason Berry wrote, "No other novelist or **historian** has provided such a shattering, human view of slavery."

But *Roots* drew criticism too. In the *New York Book Review*, Willie Lee Rose wrote that Haley had trouble developing realistic personalities for each of his many characters. The task, she wrote, "challenges Haley the artist, and **taxes** Haley the historian."

L.L. King wrote in the *Saturday Review*, "Roots, unhappily, is not the **masterwork** one had hoped for."

But in spite of the literary criticism, a new *Roots* project was ready for the public. With Haley's help, prize-winning movie producer David Wolper had made an eight-part miniseries of *Roots* for television.

Like the book, the *Roots* miniseries showed African American history from a black perspective. And, unlike most popular television shows at the time, the movie treated the characters with **dignity** and intelligence.

EXERCISE 1

SELF-TEST: After reading the above selection, do the following. Look at the Master Words below. Underline the words that you think you know. Circle the words that you are less sure about. Draw a square around the words you don't recognize.

MASTER WORDS

alter	**historian**
awareness	**manuscript**
concept	**masterwork**
dignity	**promoting**
heritage	**taxes**

Read the selection on the preceding page again, this time paying special attention to the ten Master Words. In the (a) spaces provided below, write down what you think is the meaning of the word. After you have attempted a definition for each word, look up the word in a dictionary. In the (b) spaces, copy the appropriate dictionary definition.

1. **alter** (v.)

   a. _______________________________________

   b. ___modify or adjust___________________

2. **awareness** (n.)

   a. _______________________________________

   b. ___profound knowledge or understanding___

3. **concept** (n.)

   a. _______________________________________

   b. ___abstract idea_______________________

4. **dignity** (n.)

   a. _______________________________________

   b. ___honor; esteem_______________________

5. **heritage** (n.)

   a. _______________________________________

   b. ___legacy; inherited possessions or traditions___

6. **historian** (n.)

   a. _______________________________________

   b. ___student or writer of history_______

7. **manuscript** (n.)

   a. _______________________________________

   b. ___original, typed, or handwritten text___

8. **masterwork** (n.)

   a. _______________________________________

   b. ___masterpiece; supreme achievement___

9. **promoting** (v.)

   a. _______________________________________

   b. ___calling attention to; advertising or publicizing___

10. **taxes** (v.)

    a. _______________________________________

    b. ___burdens; makes demands on__________

Use the following list of synonyms and antonyms to fill in the blanks. Some of the words have no antonyms. In such cases, the antonym blanks have been marked with an X.

advertising	disrespect	ignorance	modify
burdens	flop	legacy	original
copy	honor	maintain	student of history
degrading	idea	masterpiece	understanding

	Synonyms	**Antonyms**
1. **manuscript**	(original)	(copy)
2. **promoting**	(advertising)	(degrading)
3. **awareness**	(understanding)	(ignorance)
4. **heritage**	(legacy)	X
5. **concept**	(idea)	X
6. **alter**	(modify)	(maintain)
7. **historian**	(student of history)	X
8. **taxes**	(burdens)	X
9. **masterwork**	(masterpiece)	(flop)
10. **dignity**	(honor)	(disrespect)

Decide whether the first pair in the items below are synonyms or antonyms. Then choose the Master Word that shows a similar relation to the word(s) preceding the blank.

1. order	:chaos	::ignorance	:	(awareness)
2. repeat	:duplicate	::change	:	(alter)
3. dislike	:loathe	::text	:	(manuscript)
4. conflict	:discord	::legacy	:	(heritage)
5. instinct	:intuition	::student of history	:	(historian)
6. treasures	:trash	::dishonor	:	(dignity)
7. average	:exceptional	::degrading	:	(promoting)
8. sin	:transgression	::masterpiece	:	(masterwork)
9. tardy	:late	::idea	:	(concept)
10. refined	:elegant	::strains	:	(taxes)

The Master Words in this lesson are repeated below. From the Master Words, choose the appropriate word for the blank in each of the following sentences. Write the word in the numbered space provided at the right.

| alter | concept | heritage | manuscript | promoting |
| awareness | dignity | historian | masterwork | taxes |

1. Respect for the land and the spirit of all living things was part of their ...?... , handed down for generations.

1. _______ (heritage) _______

2. The pilots decided to ...?... their course to avoid the storm.

2. _______ (alter) _______

3. It was a new and wonderful feeling to be treated with such honor and ...?... .

3. _______ (dignity) _______

4. The artist stepped back in exhaustion and joy, admiring what she knew to be her ...?... .

4. _______ (masterwork) _______

5. The advertising campaign was their way of ...?... their product.

5. _______ (promoting) _______

6. The writer finished editing the ...?... and sent it off to the publisher.

6. _______ (manuscript) _______

7. When sales began to lag, we decided we needed a new ...?... of how to promote our products.

7. _______ (concept) _______

8. After climbing the mountain, she acquired a new ...?... of the rigors of this sport.

8. _______ (awareness) _______

9. Great physical exercise ...?... anyone who is out of shape.

9. _______ (taxes) _______

10. Even though the book on the Civil War is written by a noted ...?..., it does contain factual errors.

10. _______ (historian) _______

Using one of the Master Words, create an acrostic composition related to the meaning of the word. See the example below. Write your acrostic in the space to the right.

```
 (A)d j u s t   a
 (L)i t t l e
b i(T).
 (E)n o u g h!
P e(R)f e c t!
```

Read the following selection to get the general meaning. Read it a second time, paying special attention to the words in dark type. Notice how they are used in sentences. These are Master Words. These are the words you will be working with in this section.

from **Anne Frank: The Diary of a Young Girl** by Anne Frank

Saturday, November 28, 1942

Dearest Kitty,

We've been using too much electricity and have now exceeded our **ration**. The result: excessive **economy** and the **prospect** of having the electricity cut off. No light for fourteen days; that's a pleasant thought, isn't it? But who knows, maybe it won't be so long! It's too dark to read after four or four-thirty, so we **while** away the time with all kinds of crazy activities: telling riddles, doing **calisthenics** in the dark, speaking English or French, reviewing books—after a while everything gets boring. Yesterday I discovered a new pastime: using a good pair of binoculars to peek into the lighted rooms of the neighbors. During the day our curtains can't be opened, not even an inch, but there's no harm when it's so dark.

I never knew that neighbors could be so interesting. Ours are, at any rate. I've come across a few at dinner, one family making home movies and the dentist across the way working on a frightened old lady.

Mr. Dussel, the man who was said to get along so well with children and to absolutely adore them, has turned out to be an old-fashioned **disciplinarian** and preacher of unbearably long sermons on manners. Since I have the **singular** pleasure (!) of sharing my far too narrow room with His Excellency, and since I'm generally considered to be the worst behaved of the three young people, it's all I can do to avoid having the same old scoldings and **admonitions** repeatedly flung at my head and to pretend not to hear. This wouldn't be so bad if Mr. Dussel weren't such a tattletale and hadn't singled out Mother to be the **recipient** of his reports. If Mr. Dussel's just read me the riot act, Mother lectures me all over again, this time throwing the whole book at me. And if I'm really lucky, Mrs. van D. calls me to **account** five minutes later and lays down the law as well!

EXERCISE 1

SELF-TEST: After reading the above selection, do the following. Look at the Master Words below. Underline the words that you think you know. Circle the words that you are less sure about. Draw a square around the words you don't recognize.

MASTER WORDS

account	**prospect**
admonitions	**ration**
calisthenics	**recipient**
disciplinarian	**singular**
economy	**while**

Read the selection on the preceding page again, this time paying special attention to the ten Master Words. In the (a) spaces provided below, write down what you think is the meaning of the word. After you have attempted a definition for each word, look up the word in a dictionary. In the (b) spaces, copy the appropriate dictionary definition.

1. **account** (v.)

   a. _______________________________________

   b. _____explain one's conduct_____________

2. **admonitions** (n.)

   a. _______________________________________

   b. _____advice or warnings against faults_____

3. **calisthenics** (n.)

   a. _______________________________________

   b. _____exercises___________________________

4. **disciplinarian** (n.)

   a. _______________________________________

   b. _____one who enforces rules______________

5. **economy** (n.)

   a. _______________________________________

   b. _____careful management of money, materials, or resources so as to avoid waste_____

6. **prospect** (n.)

   a. _______________________________________

   b. _____expectation; the mental picture of something to come_____

7. **ration** (n.)

   a. _______________________________________

   b. _____a share or allowance as determined by supply_____

8. **recipient** (n.)

   a. _______________________________________

   b. _____one who receives____________________

9. **singular** (adj.)

   a. _______________________________________

   b. _____exceptional; out of the ordinary_____

10. **while** (v.)

    a. _______________________________________

    b. _____to pass pleasantly__________________

Use the following list of synonyms and antonyms to fill in the blanks. Some of the words have no antonyms. In such cases, the antonym blanks have been marked with an X.

allowance	enforcer	expectation	pass	sender
deny	exceptional	explain	ordinary	thrift
encouragement	exercises	extravagance	receiver	warnings

	Synonyms	**Antonyms**
1. **ration**	(allowance)	X
2. **economy**	(thrift)	(extravagance)
3. **prospect**	(expectation)	X
4. **while**	(pass)	X
5. **calisthenics**	(exercises)	X
6. **disciplinarian**	(enforcer)	X
7. **singular**	(exceptional)	(ordinary)
8. **admonitions**	(warnings)	(encouragement)
9. **recipient**	(receiver)	(sender)
10. **account**	(explain)	(deny)

Decide whether the first pair in the items below are synonyms or antonyms. Then choose the Master Word that shows a similar relation to the word(s) preceding the blank.

1. puny	:weak	::frugality	: (economy)
2. goal	:objective	::pass	: (while)
3. encourage	:dissuade	::sender	: (recipient)
4. friendly	:amiable	::enforcer	: (disciplinarian)
5. imaginative	:fanciful	::allowance	: (ration)
6. evaluate	:judge	::exercises	: (calisthenics)
7. severe	:lenient	::encouragement	: (admonitions)
8. timid	:fearless	::common	: (singular)
9. messenger	:courier	::likelihood	: (prospect)
10. battle	:fray	::justify	: (account)

The Master Words in this lesson are repeated below. From the Master Words, choose the appropriate word for the blank in each of the following sentences. Write the word in the numbered space provided at the right.

account	calisthenics	economy	ration	singular
admonitions	disciplinarian	prospect	recipient	while

1. It was a ...?... honor to be given this particular award.

1. ______ (singular)

2. Because he scolded the children over every little mistake, his ...?... were largely ignored.

2. ______ (admonitions)

3. Their money was running out, and so they would have to practice extreme ...?... to get through the month.

3. ______ (economy)

4. Her letter to the editor created a furor. She was the ...?... of hundreds of angry letters in response.

4. ______ (recipient)

5. The survivors in the boat knew rescue might not come soon and that they should ...?... all the food and water they had.

5. ______ (ration)

6. Before her stretched a whole day, which she was free to ...?... away as she pleased.

6. ______ (while)

7. As part of her new regimen of self-discipline, she would begin each day with ...?... and jogging.

7. ______ (calisthenics)

8. He wasn't much of a ...?... so his many dogs and cats ruled his house.

8. ______ (disciplinarian)

9. They had never flown in an airplane before, let alone visited a foreign city. This trip was a frightening ...?... .

9. ______ (prospect)

10. Kim did not have a note from her parents, so she had to ...?... for her absence from the field trip.

10. ______ (account)

Complete the crossword puzzle below.

1. limited allowance
2. enforcer of rules
3. thrift
4. exercises
5. warnings
6. expectation
7. give explanation
8. opposite of sender
9. cause to pass
10. out of the ordinary

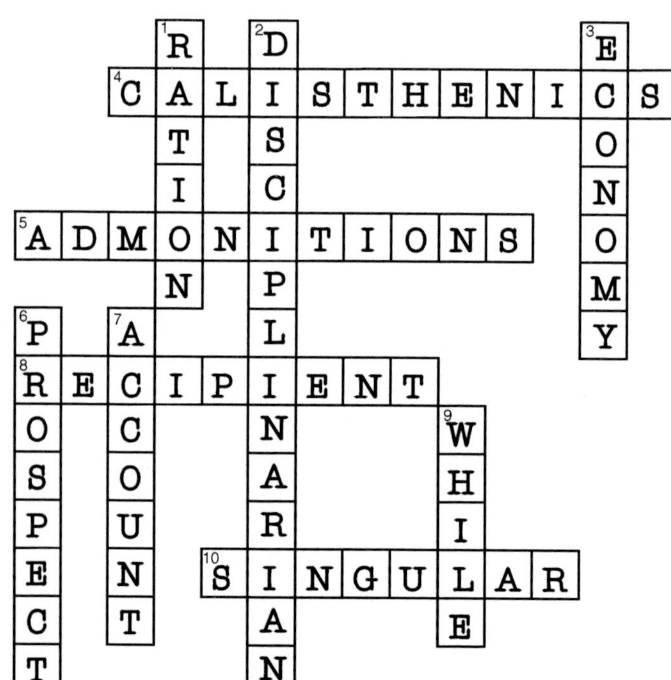

Read the following selection to get the general meaning. Read it a second time, paying special attention to the words in dark type. Notice how they are used in sentences. These are Master Words. These are the words you will be working with in this lesson.

One of the major duties of a candy-striper is to **distribute** the hospital trays at mealtimes. Once I was told to feed an old man who was unable to feed himself. At first I was unwilling to perform this task, but I finally agreed to do so.

The old man looked up as I entered his room. He must have been very old, for his loose gray skin hung in folds and **pouches** all over his arms and head. What hair he had left was very thin and white. As I approached with his tray, he followed me with his eyes but didn't speak. In fact, he never spoke.

The small bites of food I offered were accepted and soon disappeared in the small toothless mouth. **Aside** from the **mechanical** chewing, he made no movement at all. My **sympathy** went out to him, a poor old man with few years to live, if, indeed, he had any.

He seemed to take forever to finish his meal, for he **relished** every bite as if it were his very first, or last. His milky brown eyes, dull with age, stared at me **constantly** as I gave him the food.

When he finally finished, I **murmured** something polite and started to leave. As I reached the door, I **hesitated** and glanced back at him, a dying soul in an **antiseptic** prison. Although I can't be sure, I felt that underneath all his wrinkles he was smiling at me.

—Student

EXERCISE 1

SELF-TEST: After reading the above selection, do the following. Look at the Master Words below. Underline the words that you think you know. Circle the words that you are less sure about. Draw a square around the words you don't recognize.

MASTER WORDS

antiseptic	**mechanical**
aside	**murmur**
constant	**pouch**
distribute	**relish**
hesitate	**sympathy**

Read the selection on the preceding page again, this time paying special attention to the ten Master Words. In the (a) spaces provided below, write down what you think is the meaning of the word. After you have attempted a definition for each word, look up the word in a dictionary. In the (b) spaces, copy the appropriate dictionary definition.

1. **antiseptic** (adj.)

   a. _______________________________________

   b. _____ thoroughly clean ___________________

2. **aside** (adv.)

   a. _______________________________________

   b. _____ apart (from); except (for); excluding _____

3. **constant** (adj.)

   a. _______________________________________

   b. _____ continuing without a break _____________

4. **distribute** (v.)

   a. _______________________________________

   b. _____ to divide among several or many; to deal out _____

5. **hesitate** (v.)

   a. _______________________________________

   b. _____ to pause briefly, perhaps due to doubt or indecision _____

6. **mechanical** (adj.)

   a. _______________________________________

   b. _____ performed as if by a machine or from habit _____

7. **murmur** (v.)

   a. _______________________________________

   b. _____ to make a low, indistinct sound _____________

8. **pouch** (n.)

   a. _______________________________________

   b. _____ a bag or a sack _____________________

9. **relish** (v.)

   a. _______________________________________

   b. _____ to take pleasure in, especially to eat or drink with pleasure _____

10. **sympathy** (n.)

   a. _______________________________________

   b. _____ the act of entering into and sharing the feelings of another person, especially pity

Use the following list of synonyms and antonyms to fill in the blanks. Some words have no antonyms. In such cases, the antonym blanks have been marked with an X.

apart	conscious	deliver	enjoy	hardheartedness	pause
automatic	continual	dirty	gather	including	shout
bag	continue	dislike	germ-free	occasional	whisper
concern					

	Synonyms	**Antonyms**
1. **distribute**	(deliver)	(gather)
2. **pouch**	(bag)	X
3. **aside**	(apart)	(including)
4. **mechanical**	(automatic)	(conscious)
5. **sympathy**	(concern)	(hardheartedness)
6. **relish**	(enjoy)	(dislike)
7. **constant**	(continual)	(occasional)
8. **murmur**	(whisper)	(shout)
9. **hesitate**	(pause)	(continue)
10. **antiseptic**	(germ-free)	(dirty)

Decide whether the first pair in the items below are synonyms or antonyms. Then choose the Master Word that shows a similar relation to the word(s) preceding the blank.

1. canter	:jog	::wait	: (hesitate)
2. anxious	:calm	::yell	: (murmur)
3. disabled	:able-bodied	::hate	: (relish)
4. dappled	:blotchy	::robotlike	: (mechanical)
5. fidgety	:relaxed	::collect	: (distribute)
6. despondent	:merry	::mockery	: (sympathy)
7. breeding	:education	::sack	: (pouch)
8. remarkable	:average	::irregular	: (constant)
9. dun	:muddy	::sterile	: (antiseptic)
10. shuffle	:drag	::except	: (aside)

The Master Words in this lesson are repeated below. From the Master Words, choose the appropriate word for the blank in each of the following sentences. Write the word in the numbered space provided at the right.

| antiseptic | constant | hesitate | murmur | relish |
| aside | distribute | mechanical | pouch | sympathy |

1. ...?... from the tax issue, I found myself in agreement with the candidate's major policies.

1. _______ (aside)

2. In an operating room everything must be ...?... so that a patient will not catch a disease.

2. _______ (antiseptic)

3. Correct use of the ZIP code helps postal workers to ...?... the mail.

3. _______ (distribute)

4. A baby kangaroo, about the size of a bee when it's born, spends four to five months in its mother's ...?...

4. _______ (pouch)

5. Mother's answer was ...?...; she hadn't listened to my question.

5. _______ (mechanical)

6. I was standing close enough to hear Regina ...?... a reply.

6. _______ (murmur)

7. The quarterback ...?...(d, ed) for a long moment before finally passing the ball to Lance.

7. _______ (hesitate)

8. A ...?... driving rain resulted in flood waters, which spilled into the Nishna Valley.

8. _______ (constant)

9. The ...?... of my friends helped me get over the disappointment of not winning the contest.

9. _______ (sympathy)

10. Students often ...?... the thought of vacation, only to find that they don't have enough activities to fill their leisure hours.

10. _______ (relish)

To complete this puzzle, fill in the Master Word associated with each phrase below. Then unscramble the circled letters to form a Master Word from Lesson 2, and define it.

1. to pause in doubt — h (e) s i t a t e

2. what postal carriers do with the mail — d (i) s t r i b u t e

3. apart from that — a s (i) d e

4. cleaner than clean — a n (t) i s e p t i c

5. you might feel this for a friend who is ill — s y m (p) a t h y

6. all the time — c o (n) s t a n t

7. lick your lips — (r) e l i s h

8. like a puppet's movements — m (e) c h a n i c a l

9. this can be a purse or a knapsack — p o u (c) h

Unscrambled word: (recipient)

Definition: (one who gets; receiver)

(Note: Definition may vary.)

Read the following selection to get the general meaning. Read it a second time, paying special attention to the words in dark type. Notice how they are used in sentences. These are Master Words. These are the words you will be working with in this lesson.

Adapted from **Through the Looking-Glass**
by Lewis Carroll

"I see nobody on the road," said Alice.

"I only wish *I* had such eyes," the King remarked in a **fretful** tone. "To be able to see Nobody! And at that distance too! Why, it's as much as *I* can do to see real people, by this light!"

All this was lost on Alice, who was still looking **intently** along the road, shading her eyes with one hand. "I see somebody now!" she exclaimed at last. "But he's coming very slowly — and what curious **attitudes** he goes into!" (For the Messenger kept skipping up and down, and **wriggling** like an eel, as he came along, with his great hands spread out like fans on each side.)

The Messenger, to Alice's great amusement, opened a bag that hung round his neck, and handed a sandwich to the King, who **devoured** it **greedily**.

"Another sandwich!" said the King.

"There's nothing but hay left now," the Messenger said, peeping into the bag.

"Hay, then," the king murmured in a faint whisper.

Alice was glad to see that it [**refreshed**] him a good deal. "There's nothing like eating hay when you're faint," he remarked to her, as he **munched** away.

"I should think throwing cold water over you would be better," Alice suggested.

"I didn't say there was nothing *better*," the King replied. "I said there was nothing *like* it." Which Alice did not **venture** to **deny**.

EXERCISE 1

SELF-TEST: After reading the above selection, do the following. Look at the Master Words below. Underline the words that you think you know. Circle the words that you are less sure about. Draw a square around the words you don't recognize.

MASTER WORDS

attitude	**intent**
deny	**munch**
devour	**refresh**
fretful	**venture**
greedily	**wriggle**

Read the selection on the preceding page again, this time paying special attention to the ten Master Words. In the (a) spaces provided below, write down what you think is the meaning of the word. After you have attempted a definition for each word, look up the word in a dictionary. In the (b) spaces, copy the appropriate dictionary definition.

1. **attitude** (n.)

   a. ____

   b. _______ posture; physical position of the body _______

2. **deny** (v.)

   a. ____

   b. _______ to declare that something is untrue _______

3. **devour** (v.)

   a. ____

   b. _______ to eat quickly and hungrily _______

4. **fretful** (adj.)

   a. ____

   b. _______ irritable; worried; discontented; impatient _______

5. **greedily** (adv.)

   a. ____

   b. _______ eagerly; ravenously _______

6. **intent** (adj.)

   a. ____

   b. _______ directed with eager or fixed attention _______

7. **munch** (v.)

   a. ____

   b. _______ to chew steadily or vigorously, often with a crunching sound _______

8. **refresh** (v.)

   a. ____

   b. _______ to restore strength or spirit to; to revive or put new life into _______

9. **venture** (v.)

   a. ____

   b. _______ to dare to say at the risk of criticism, argument, etc. _______

10. **wriggle** (v.)

   a. ____

   b. _______ to twist to and fro; to squirm _______

Use the following list of synonyms and antonyms to fill in the blanks. Some words have no antonyms. In such cases, the antonym blanks have been marked with an X.

absent-minded	chew	disclaim	irritable	relaxed
absorbed	consume	exhaust	politely	renew
admit	dare	hungrily	position	squirm
avoid				

	Synonyms	**Antonyms**
1. **fretful**	(irritable)	(relaxed)
2. **intent**	(absorbed)	(absent-minded)
3. **attitude**	(position)	X
4. **wriggle**	(squirm)	X
5. **devour**	(consume)	X
6. **greedily**	(hungrily)	(politely)
7. **refresh**	(renew)	(exhaust)
8. **munch**	(chew)	X
9. **venture**	(dare)	(avoid)
10. **deny**	(disclaim)	(admit)

Decide whether the first pair in the items below are synonyms or antonyms. Then choose the Master Word that shows a similar relation to the word(s) preceding the blank.

1. murmur	:scream	::agree with	:	(deny)
2. hesitate	:delay	::nibble	:	(munch)
3. mechanical	:unconscious	::pose	:	(attitude)
4. relish	:delight in	::interested	:	(intent)
5. pouch	:purse	::gobble	:	(devour)
6. distribute	:circulate	::selfishly	:	(greedily)
7. sympathy	:indifference	::tire	:	(refresh)
8. antiseptic	:disinfected	::twist	:	(wriggle)
9. aside	:besides	::attempt	:	(venture)
10. constant	:now and then	::calm	:	(fretful)

The Master Words in this lesson are repeated below. From the Master Words, choose the appropriate word for the blank in each of the following sentences. Write the word in the numbered space provided at the right.

attitude	devour	greedily	munch	venture
deny	fretful	intent	refresh	wriggle

1. The travelers ...?...(d, ed) themselves at the cool well before continuing their journey through the desert.

1. ________ (refresh)

2. The reckless ...?... of the man on the tightrope made the audience laugh and gasp.

2. ________ (attitude)

3. It doesn't bother me when my roommate quietly eats his yogurt, but I can't study when he begins to ...?... on potato chips.

3. ________ (munch)

4. All of us were too embarrassed to ask except for Meg, who ...?...(d, ed) the question without a blush.

4. ________ (venture)

5. When a ten-foot snake uncoils, its tail soon begins to ...?... .

5. ________ (wriggle)

6. The selfish little boy ...?... ate the pizza without offering his friends a bite.

6. ________ (greedily)

7. The suspect did not ...?... that he had been in the store on the night of the crime, but he did swear he was not the robber.

7. ________ (deny)

8. Robert was able to ...?... three gallons of ice cream in fourteen minutes during the Fourth of July celebration.

8. ________ (devour)

9. When one person in a family is short-tempered, others, too, may soon become ...?... .

9. ________ (fretful)

10. Shelley was ...?... upon her sewing as she hurried to finish her new shirt for the party.

10. ________ (intent)

To complete the crossword, choose the Master Word associated with each word or phrase below. Begin each answer in the square having the same number as the clue.

1. cold lemonade will do this on a hot day

2. "chow down"

3. move like a worm on a hook

4. you might eat this way after a day without food

5. you do this when you eat popcorn

6. to take a chance

7. uneasy and restless

8. someone focused on a task is this

9. "I did not!"

10. body position

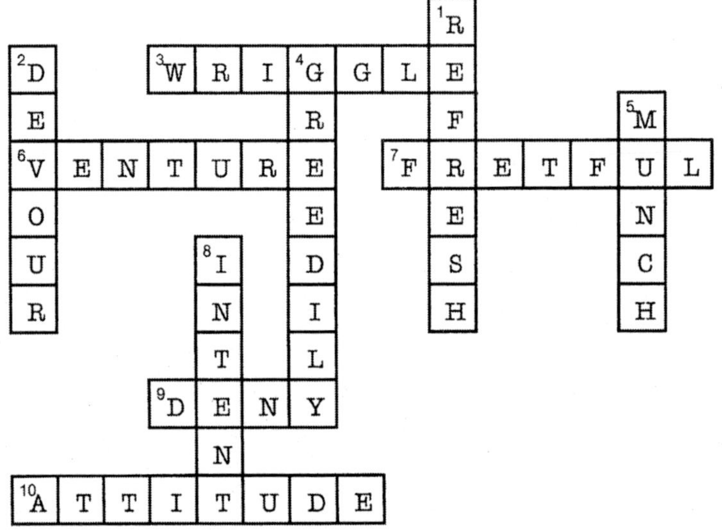

Read the following selection to get the general meaning. Read it a second time, paying special attention to the words in dark type. Notice how they are used in sentences. These are Master Words. These are the words you will be working with in this lesson.

From **Twenty Thousand Leagues Under the Sea** by Jules Verne

. . . Everything was frozen—even the noise. The *Nautilus* was then **obliged** to stop in its **adventurous** course amid these fields of ice. In spite of our efforts, in spite of the powerful means **employed** to break up the ice, the *Nautilus* remained **immovable**. Generally, when we can proceed no further, we have return still open to us; but here return was as impossible as advance, for every pass had closed behind us; . . . I was obliged to admit that Captain Nemo was more than **imprudent**. I was on the platform at that moment. The Captain had been observing our situation for some time past, when he said to me—

"Well, sir, what do you think of this?"

"I think that we are caught, Captain."

"So, M. Aronnax, you really think that the *Nautilus* cannot **disengage** itself?"

"With difficulty, Captain; for the season is already too far advanced for you to [**rely**] on the breaking up of the ice."

"Ah! sir," said Captain Nemo, in an **ironical** tone, "you will always be the same. You see nothing but difficulties and **obstacles**. I **affirm** that not only can the *Nautilus* disengage itself, but also that it can go further still."

"Further to the south?" I asked, looking at the Captain.

"Yes, sir; it shall go to the pole."

EXERCISE 1

SELF-TEST: After reading the above selection, do the following. Look at the Master Words below. Underline the words that you think you know. Circle the words that you are less sure about. Draw a square around the words you don't recognize.

MASTER WORDS

adventurous	**imprudent**
affirm	**ironical**
disengage	**oblige**
employ	**obstacle**
immovable	**rely**

Read the selection on the preceding page again, this time paying special attention to the ten Master Words. In the (a) spaces provided below, write down what you think is the meaning of the word. After you have attempted a definition for each word, look up the word in a dictionary. In the (b) spaces, copy the appropriate dictionary definition.

1. **adventurous** (adj.)

   a. _______________________________________

   b. _____ involving a risk; courageous _______

2. **affirm** (v.)

   a. _______________________________________

   b. _____ to declare something to be true or factual _____

3. **disengage** (v.)

   a. _______________________________________

   b. _____ to release or detach; to set free _____

4. **employ** (v.)

   a. _______________________________________

   b. _____ to make use of _______

5. **immovable** (adj.)

   a. _______________________________________

   b. _____ incapable of being moved; fixed; stationary; motionless _____

6. **imprudent** (adj.)

   a. _______________________________________

   b. _____ lacking caution and good judgment; rash; unwise _____

7. **ironical** (adj.)

   a. _______________________________________

   b. _____ mocking or sarcastic; implying the opposite of what is said or written _____

8. **oblige** (v.)

   a. _______________________________________

   b. _____ to force as a result of circumstances; to bind or obligate _____

9. **obstacle** (n.)

   a. _______________________________________

   b. _____ that which stands in the way; a barrier _____

10. **rely** (v.)

   a. _______________________________________

   b. _____ to count on; to depend on; also, to trust _____

Use the following list of synonyms and antonyms to fill in the blanks. Some words have no antonyms. In such cases, the antonym blanks have been marked with an X.

aid   deny   movable   require   sincere   unwise
barrier   depend   permit   satirical   stuck   use
bind   discard   release   sensible   timid   vow
daring   distrust

	Synonyms	**Antonyms**
1. **oblige**	(require)	(permit) (release)
2. **adventurous**	(daring)	(timid)
3. **employ**	(use)	(discard)
4. **immovable**	(stuck)	(movable)
5. **imprudent**	(unwise)	(sensible)
6. **disengage**	(release)	(bind)
7. **rely**	(depend)	(distrust)
8. **ironical**	(satirical)	(sincere)
9. **obstacle**	(barrier)	(aid)
10. **affirm**	(vow)	(deny)

Decide whether the first pair in the items below are synonyms or antonyms. Then choose the Master Word that shows a similar relation to the word(s) preceding the blank.

1. munch	:gnaw	::loosen	:	(disengage)
2. attitude	:posture	::try out	:	(employ)
3. devour	:gulp	::trust	:	(rely)
4. deny	:reject	::force	:	(oblige)
5. intent	:bored	::portable	:	(immovable)
6. wriggle	:wiggle	::hurdle	:	(obstacle)
7. greedily	:moderately	::wise	:	(imprudent)
8. venture	:try	::bold	:	(adventurous)
9. refresh	:weary	::doubt	:	(affirm)
10. fretful	:peaceful	::serious	:	(ironical)

    LESSON FIVE

The Master Words in this lesson are repeated below. From the Master Words, choose the appropriate word for the blank in each of the following sentences. Write the word in the numbered space provided at the right.

adventurous	disengage	immovable	ironical	obstacle
affirm	employ	imprudent	oblige	rely

1. The hurdler cleared every ...?... on the track and won the race.

   1. ______ (obstacle) ______

2. The voyages to the moon were exciting and ...?... missions.

   2. ______ (adventurous) ______

3. Although the worried parents ...?...(d, ed) all means available to them, they could find no trace of their missing daughter.

   3. ______ (employ) ______

4. The candidate could ...?... on the support of only 932 delegates; it would be an open convention.

   4. ______ (rely) ______

5. Union leaders remained ...?... in their demand for higher wages no matter what management said.

   5. ______ (immovable) ______

6. We realized we would have to call a wrecker to ...?... the two locked bumpers.

   6. ______ (disengage) ______

7. You must learn to determine when speakers or writers are being ...?... and when they are being straightforward.

   7. ______ (ironical) ______

8. Because the bridge was gone, the men were ...?...(d, ed) to find another way across the river.

   8. ______ (oblige) ______

9. Though no one believed the poor woman, she ...?...(d, ed) over and over that she was once wealthy.

   9. ______ (affirm) ______

10. Riding a bicycle at night without adequate lights and reflectors is nothing short of ...?... .

    10. ______ (imprudent) ______

Write the Master Word that is associated with each word group below. Then list three things that might be associated with the review word that follows.

1. steeplechase, problem, roadblock ______ (obstacle) ______

2. unbolt, disconnect, free ______ (disengage) ______

3. operate, practice, handle ______ (employ) ______

4. drunk driving, gambling, stealing ______ (imprudent) ______

5. skydiving, bullfighting, mountain climbing ______ (adventurous) ______

6. North Star, Old Faithful, Rock of Gibraltar ______ (immovable) ______

7. pledges, beliefs, sermons ______ (affirm) ______

8. contracts, treaties, promises ______ (oblige) ______

9. satire, jabs, puns ______ (ironical) ______

10. gravity, friends, alarm clocks ______ (rely) ______

Review word: shuffle (Lesson 2)

______ (feet) ______   ______ (cards) ______   ______ (papers) ______

(Note: Answers may vary.)

LESSON 6

Read the following selection to get the general meaning. Read it a second time, paying special attention to the words in dark type. Notice how they are used in sentences. These are Master Words. These are the words you will be working with in this lesson.

From **Durango Street**
by Frank Bonham

Mr. Rubio **chuckled** and blew a speck of paper from his desk **blotter**. "I hear you're a crew leader now," he said. "How do you like the job?"

Rufus grinned. "Fine. When I say 'frog,' those cats better jump."

Mr. Rubio wiggled a pencil **reflectively**. "What if a cat didn't jump?" he asked. "What would you do?"

Rufus smelled another of the sly **gambits** with which he was always trying to get him to explain why he had stolen and wrecked that automobile and got himself shipped to Pine Valley. But inside Rufus's mind was one place they were not going—not today, not tomorrow, not next year. So he merely **shrugged** and looked out the window again.

The social worker wrote something on a paper in Rufus's folder. "You haven't had many letters from your mother since you came here, it seems to me," he said thoughtfully.

"No. My old lady would rather lose a tooth than write a letter."

"Lots of people hate to write letters. I'm glad you understand that, and that your feelings aren't hurt."

Something about the statement **irritated** Rufus. He **gazed** unblinking across the desk.

"Why should my feelings be hurt?" he said. "That's stupid, letting anybody get at you that way. I've got twenty kids in my crew, and some cat's always giving me a hard time—trying to make a fool of me in front of the gang. But ol' Rufus stays on top of things. Let somebody else get his feelings hurt—I got too much to do."

Mr. Rubio nodded seriously. "Excellent **philosophy**," he said. "In fact—" Then he hesitated. Rufus **suspected** that he wanted to move quickly to another subject, but felt he must do it smoothly. He wiggled his pencil again and finally said:

"In a way, that ability to stay on top of things is the difference between a bench warmer and a first-string halfback. Wouldn't you say?"

In Rufus's mind a red light flashed beside the tracks. Last week, too, Mr. Rubio had mentioned football. And both times he had talked about halfbacks!

Now, that was more than **coincidence**.

"I guess you're right," he said calmly.

EXERCISE 1

SELF-TEST: After reading the above selection, do the following. Look at the Master Words below. Underline the words that you think you know. Circle the words that you are less sure about. Draw a square around the words you don't recognize.

MASTER WORDS

blotter	**gaze**	**reflective**
chuckle	**irritate**	**shrug**
coincidence	**philosophy**	**suspect**
gambit		

21

Read the selection on the preceding page again, this time paying special attention to the ten Master Words. In the (a) spaces provided below, write down what you think is the meaning of the word. After you have attempted a definition for each word, look up the word in a dictionary. In the (b) spaces, copy the appropriate dictionary definition.

1. **blotter** (n.)

   a. ______________________________

   b. paper used for absorbing excess ink

2. **chuckle** (v.)

   a. ______________________________

   b. to laugh quietly to oneself, often with the feeling of satisfaction

3. **coincidence** (n.)

   a. ______________________________

   b. an unusual occurrence of two or more events at one time, apparently by chance

4. **gambit** (n.)

   a. ______________________________

   b. a maneuver by which one intends to gain an advantage over an opponent

5. **gaze** (v.)

   a. ______________________________

   b. to look at steadily or intently

6. **irritate** (v.)

   a. ______________________________

   b. to cause one to be impatient, angry, or displeased; to bother or annoy

7. **philosophy** (n.)

   a. ______________________________

   b. a system of principles for guidance in daily living

8. **reflective** (adj.)

   a. ______________________________

   b. thoughtful; pondering; meditative

9. **shrug** (v.)

   a. ______________________________

   b. to raise and lower the shoulders, often expressing uncertainty or indifference

10. **suspect** (v.)

    a. ______________________________

    b. to imagine something to be true or likely

Use the following list of synonyms and antonyms to fill in the blanks. Some words have no antonyms. In such cases, the antonym blanks have been marked with an X.

chance   know   pad   shake   tactic
cry   laugh   peek   soothe   thoughtful
disturb   outlook   plan   stare   unthinking
guess

	Synonyms	**Antonyms**
1. **chuckle**	(laugh)	(cry)
2. **blotter**	(pad)	X
3. **reflective**	(thoughtful)	(unthinking)
4. **gambit**	(tactic)	X
5. **shrug**	(shake)	X
6. **irritate**	(disturb)	(soothe)
7. **gaze**	(stare)	(peek)
8. **philosophy**	(outlook)	X
9. **suspect**	(guess)	(know)
10. **coincidence**	(chance)	(plan)

Decide whether the first pair in the items below are synonyms or antonyms. Then choose the Master Word that shows a similar relation to the word(s) preceding the blank.

1. oblige	:excuse	::design	: (coincidence)
2. immovable	:mobile	::impulsive	: (reflective)
3. disengage	:untie	::look at	: (gaze)
4. employ	:utilize	::strategy	: (gambit)
5. imprudent	:practical	::weep	: (chuckle)
6. rely	:count on	::raise and lower	: (shrug)
7. affirm	:declare	::suppose	: (suspect)
8. obstacle	:roadblock	::absorbent paper	: (blotter)
9. adventurous	:heroic	::viewpoint	: (philosophy)
10. ironical	:straightforward	::please	: (irritate)

The Master Words in this lesson are repeated below. From the Master Words, choose the appropriate word for the blank in each of the following sentences. Write the word in the numbered space provided at the right.

| blotter | coincidence | gaze | philosophy | shrug |
| chuckle | gambit | irritate | reflective | suspect |

1. The ...?... Julian lived by was to take one day at a time.

1. _____ (philosophy)

2. The principal became angry when the pupil continued to ...?... in response to his questions.

2. _____ (shrug)

3. That I had $4.05 in my wallet—the exact cost of my purchase— was a lucky ...?... .

3. _____ (coincidence)

4. A secondary function of (a, an) ...?... is to protect the surface of a desk from being scratched.

4. _____ (blotter)

5. Grandma opened the chess game with a bold ...?..., and John could feel himself on the defensive already.

5. _____ (gambit)

6. Although he ...?...(d, ed) after the speeding car, the policeman was unable to read the license number.

6. _____ (gaze)

7. I have no proof, but I ...?... Ken broke my car window.

7. _____ (suspect)

8. The puppy's amusing tricks made us all smile and ...?... .

8. _____ (chuckle)

9. Mary continued to practice her piano lesson; the repetition of so few notes began to ...?... everyone in the room.

9. _____ (irritate)

10. Whenever I finish a book, I spend a few ...?... moments relating what I read to my own life.

10. _____ (reflective)

Fill in the chart below with the Master Word that fits each set of clues. Part of speech refers to the word's usage in the lesson. Use a dictionary when necessary.

Number of Syllables	Part of Speech	Other Clues		Master Word
2	noun	also a chess move	1.	(gambit)
3	adjective	in a thinking mood	2.	(reflective)
2	verb	you do this when tickled	3.	(chuckle)
3	verb	delays or insults may do this	4.	(irritate)
1	verb	this gesture may mean "I don't know"	5.	(shrug)
2	noun	it soaks up ink	6.	(blotter)
4	noun	Greek root means "loving"	7.	(philosophy)
2	verb	what a Doubting Thomas does	8.	(suspect)
1	verb	you might do this on starry nights	9.	(gaze)
4	noun	being born and dying on the same day is an example	10.	(coincidence)

Read the following selection to get the general meaning. Read it a second time, paying special attention to the words in dark type. Notice how they are used in sentences. These are Master Words. These are the words you will be working with in this lesson.

From **"Why Banks Is Robbed in Texas"**
by Henry Gregor Felsen

In Texas, Curly Kid was used to riding the open plains until he came to a place where there was a little string of saloons and stores on one side of the trail, and another little string of saloons and stores on the other, and that was town. And the only difference between the big towns and the little towns, was that the big towns [were] somewhat longer than the little towns. And he was **expert** at riding into one end of a town, robbing the bank, shooting anybody that moved, and riding out the other end with a **posse** hot on his heels. And, naturally, he had **assumed** that he would follow this proven method of robbery in Oklahoma City—the moment he discovered which side of the street the bank was on.

But . . . ! Instead of following the natural, rightful Texas **pattern**, [those] dumb Oklahomans had built a dozen or more streets all running side by side in the same direction; which was about the silliest **duplication** of effort Curly Kid had ever seen. And, to make matters worse, they had allowed a whole mess of streets to spring up that **intersected** with these first streets.

As a result of this lack of planning, there was a big **junction** every hundred yards or so, jammed with people and horses and wagons and cattle, all trying to cross the same piece of ground, in different directions, and at the same time. Naturally, it couldn't be done.

It was a **marvel** to Curly Kid how people living so close to Texas could have such strange ways, and he could have watched for hours, chuckling and **exclaiming** to himself over the **antics** of [those] crazy Oklahomans. But he had business to attend to, and he was too serious about his work to let entertainment interfere with it for more than a minute.

EXERCISE 1

SELF-TEST: After reading the above selection, do the following. Look at the Master Words below. Underline the words that you think you know. Circle the words that you are less sure about. Draw a square around the words you don't recognize.

MASTER WORDS

antics	**intersect**
assume	**junction**
duplication	**marvel**
exclaim	**pattern**
expert	**posse**

25

Read the selection on the preceding page again, this time paying special attention to the ten Master Words. In the (a) spaces provided below, write down what you think is the meaning of the word. After you have attempted a definition for each word, look up the word in a dictionary. In the (b) spaces, copy the appropriate dictionary definition.

1. **antics** (n.)

   a. ____

   b. _____ humorous, strange, or fantastic gestures, positions, or tricks

2. **assume** (v.)

   a. ____

   b. _____ to take for granted; to suppose

3. **duplication** (n.)

   a. ____

   b. _____ a thing identical to something else; a replica or copy

4. **exclaim** (v.)

   a. ____

   b. _____ to cry out or speak loudly, as from surprise or strong emotion

5. **expert** (adj.)

   a. ____

   b. _____ having special skill, knowledge, or training

6. **intersect** (v.)

   a. ____

   b. _____ to meet or join by passing through or across

7. **junction** (n.)

   a. ____

   b. _____ a place where things, such as railroads, streets, or rivers, come together

8. **marvel** (n.)

   a. ____

   b. _____ something that causes wonder or amazement

9. **pattern** (n.)

   a. ____

   b. _____ a design or arrangement; also, a model or guide

10. **posse** (n.)

   a. ____

   b. _____ a group of persons with legal power to help a sheriff keep the peace

Use the following list of synonyms and antonyms to fill in the blanks. Some words have no antonyms. In such cases, the antonym blanks have been marked with an X.

amateurish	crossroads	know	outlaws	shout	tricks
commonplace	design	lawmen	parallel	skillful	whisper
copy	disorder	original	separation	suppose	wonder
cross					

	Synonyms	**Antonyms**
1. **expert**	(skillful)	(amateurish)
2. **posse**	(lawmen)	(outlaws)
3. **assume**	(suppose)	(know)
4. **pattern**	(design)	(disorder)
5. **duplication**	(copy)	(original)
6. **intersect**	(cross)	(parallel)
7. **junction**	(crossroads) (cross)	(separation)
8. **marvel**	(wonder)	(commonplace)
9. **exclaim**	(shout)	(whisper)
10. **antics**	(tricks)	X

Decide whether the first pair in the items below are synonyms or antonyms. Then choose the Master Word that shows a similar relation to the word(s) preceding the blank.

1. gaze	:watch	::believe	: (assume)
2. gambit	:move	::foolishness	: (antics)
3. coincidence	:scheme	::murmur	: (exclaim)
4. shrug	:toss	::outline	: (pattern)
5. reflective	:concentrating	::amazement	: (marvel)
6. blotter	:pad	::crossing	: (junction)
7. philosophy	:beliefs	::connect	: (intersect)
8. chuckle	:sob	::unskilled	: (expert)
9. suspect	:confirm	::one-of-a-kind	: (duplication)
10. irritate	:calm	::criminals	: (posse)

The Master Words in this lesson are repeated below. From the Master Words, choose the appropriate word for the blank in each of the following sentences. Write the word in the numbered space provided at the right.

antics	duplication	expert	junction	pattern
assume	exclaim	intersect	marvel	posse

1. Thousands of tourists come to the Grand Canyon each year to gaze and wonder at one of nature's greatest ...?...(s).

1. _______ (marvel) _______

2. Major cities often spring up at the ...?... of two rivers.

2. _______ (junction) _______

3. The ...?... of the clown as he pranced around the ring were a delight to young and old alike.

3. _______ (antics) _______

4. Photocopying machines have made the ...?... of important papers a simple matter.

4. _______ (duplication) _______

5. Only the most ...?... mathematicians could solve the difficult problem.

5. _______ (expert) _______

6. Members of the drill team marched across the field in two lines which would ...?... at midfield.

6. _______ (intersect) _______

7. Oriental rugs are known for their fine workmanship and detailed ...?...(s).

7. _______ (pattern) _______

8. I ...?... Paul and Sue will be married soon after their engagement.

8. _______ (assume) _______

9. The sheriff rounded up (a, an) ...?... to help him track the bank robbers.

9. _______ (posse) _______

10. As Paul Revere rode through New England towns, he ...?...(d, ed), "The British are coming!"

10. _______ (exclaim) _______

Use at least five Master Words from this lesson to write a scene about one of the following topics. Or create a topic of your own. Write your choice on the blank. Circle the Master Words as you use them.

Possible Topics: Wandering Through a Foreign City, Incident at the Crossroads

____

____

____

____

____

____

____

(Note: Answers will vary.)

Read the following selection to get the general meaning. Read it a second time, paying special attention to the words in dark type. Notice how they are used in sentences. These are Master Words. These are the words you will be working with in this lesson.

The sign in the restaurant window read, "All Help Needed." John's spirits rose and the **despair** he had felt for months suddenly lifted. He opened the door of the restaurant and was greeted by the smiling face of the **maitre d'**. "Table, sir?"

John was so anxious that his words ran together. "Sir, I saw the sign, you know, I need a job and wondered if I could speak to the manager . . ."

The maitre d' looked more closely at John and his smile disappeared. "Yes, well, come along, then. I'm not certain that there are any jobs left."

"But I saw a sign."

"Yes, but it's been up for weeks and there have been many **applicants**. The manager should have taken the sign down days ago."

John was still hopeful as the maitre d' led him down a long hallway toward the manager's office. The manager would be the one to do the hiring.

The maitre d' knocked on the manager's door. "Come in," barked a voice. The maitre d' opened the door and John followed him into the room.

The manager sat **tilted** back in his chair with his shoes **propped** upon his otherwise bare desk. He was a tall, thin man with a hooked nose and arched brows over eyes that stared at John with **suspicion**.

"Mr. Jenson, this boy is looking for a job. I told him that there have been many applicants, and that it was **entirely** my fault the sign was still up."

The manager closed the magazine he was reading, leaving his bony forefinger between the pages to keep his place. The maitre d' left, closing the door gently behind him.

"I'm afraid he's right, son. I'm sorry that the sign was still up and **misled** you. Do you want to write down your name and address?"

Dutifully, John wrote out his name and address on the note pad. He managed to say a polite thanks and headed for the door. As he closed the door, he realized he had forgotten to leave his phone number.

When he opened the manager's door, Mr. Jenson was once again leafing carelessly through the magazine. On the corner of the desk lay a **crumpled** piece of note pad paper.

—Student

EXERCISE 1

SELF-TEST: After reading the above selection, do the following. Look at the Master Words below. Underline the words that you think you know. Circle the words that you are less sure about. Draw a square around the words you don't recognize.

MASTER WORDS

applicant	**entirely**	**prop**
crumple	**maitre d'**	**suspicion**
despair	**mislead**	**tilt**
dutiful		

Read the selection on the preceding page again, this time paying special attention to the ten Master Words. In the (a) spaces provided below, write down what you think is the meaning of the word. After you have attempted a definition for each word, look up the word in a dictionary. In the (b) spaces, copy the appropriate dictionary definition.

1. **applicant** (n.)

    a. ____

    b. _____ one who applies for or requests a job, help, etc.; a candidate

2. **crumple** (v.)

    a. ____

    b. _____ to crush together into folds or wrinkles; to rumple

3. **despair** (n.)

    a. ____

    b. _____ complete loss of hope, faith, or confidence

4. **dutiful** (adj.)

    a. ____

    b. _____ having a sense of duty or obligation; obedient; respectful

5. **entirely** (adv.)

    a. ____

    b. _____ wholly; fully; in all respects

6. **maitre d'** (n.)

    a. ____

    b. _____ the headwaiter in a restaurant

7. **mislead** (v.)

    a. ____

    b. _____ to lead into error of conduct or thought; to lead astray

8. **prop** (v.)

    a. ____

    b. _____ to prevent something from falling by placing something under or against it; also, to rest upon such a support

9. **suspicion** (n.)

    a. ____

    b. _____ the feeling that something is wrong; uneasiness; distrust

10. **tilt** (v.)

    a. ____

    b. _____ to cause to lean, incline, slope, or slant

Use the following list of synonyms and antonyms to fill in the blanks. Some words have no antonyms. In such cases, the antonym blanks have been marked with an X.

busboy	deceive	guide	lean	rebellious	support
candidate	distrust	headwaiter	obedient	smooth	tumble
completely	employer	hopelessness	partly	straighten	wrinkle
confidence	faith				

	Synonyms	**Antonyms**
1. **despair**	(hopelessness)	(faith)
2. **maitre d'**	(headwaiter)	(busboy)
3. **applicant**	(candidate)	(employer)
4. **tilt**	(lean)	(straighten)
5. **prop**	(support)	(tumble)
6. **suspicion**	(distrust)	(confidence)
7. **entirely**	(completely)	(partly)
8. **mislead**	(deceive)	(guide)
9. **dutiful**	(obedient)	(rebellious)
10. **crumple**	(wrinkle)	(smooth)

EXERCISE 4 ▮▮▮▮▮▮▮▮▮▮▮▮▮▮▮▮▮▮▮▮▮▮▮▮▮▮▮▮▮▮

Decide whether the first pair in the items below are synonyms or antonyms. Then choose the Master Word that shows a similar relation to the word(s) preceding the blank.

1. assume	:presuppose	::slant	: (tilt)
2. exclaim	:mumble	::flatten	: (crumple)
3. marvel	:routine matter	::interviewer	: (applicant)
4. expert	:untrained	::trust	: (suspicion)
5. duplication	:reproduction	::respectful	: (dutiful)
6. antics	:pranks	::brace	: (prop)
7. pattern	:model	::totally	: (entirely)
8. junction	:crossroads	::chief waiter	: (maitre d')
9. intersect	:crisscross	::misinform	: (mislead)
10. posse	:fugitive	::hope	: (despair)

The Master Words in this lesson are repeated below. From the Master Words, choose the appropriate word for the blank in each of the following sentences. Write the word in the numbered space provided at the right.

| applicant | despair | entirely | mislead | suspicion |
| crumple | dutiful | maitre d' | prop | tilt |

1. Bob nervously realized that he was not the only ...?... for the job.

1. _____ (applicant)

2. The couple was disappointed that the ...?... had not seated them near a window.

2. _____ (maitre d')

3. After searching the closet, I finally found my favorite blouse ...?...(d, ed) on the floor.

3. _____ (crumple)

4. The Leaning Tower of Pisa is famous because its poor foundation caused it to ...?... even before it was completely built.

4. _____ (tilt)

5. The ...?... of the fans was obvious as their team lost its fourth game in a row.

5. _____ (despair)

6. Kevin brought two books to ...?... up the movie projector so the image on the screen would be square.

6. _____ (prop)

7. Advertising often ...?...(s) consumers into thinking that a particular product will solve many problems.

7. _____ (mislead)

8. The ...?... dog would sit for hours on command.

8. _____ (dutiful)

9. The con man first roused my ...?... by insisting that he had to have cash for his goods.

9. _____ (suspicion)

10. Her arguments weren't ...?... convincing, so he asked for more proof.

10. _____ (entirely)

EXERCISE 6 ◼◼◼◼◼◼◼◼◼◼◼◼◼◼

To complete this puzzle, fill in the Master Word associated with each phrase below. Then unscramble the circled letters to form a Master Word from Lesson 7, and define it.

1. what clothes do if you sleep in them — c r u m p l e

2. you have this if you "smell a rat" — s u s p i (c) i o n

3. what some book covers do — m i s l e (a) d

4. loyal and considerate — d u (t) i f u l

5. tell this person if the service isn't good — m a (i) t r e d'

6. result of being "down in the dumps" — d e (s) p a i r

7. one hundred percent — e (n) t i r e l y

8. future employee, perhaps — a p p l i c a n t

9. to rest against — p r o p

10. how to straighten a crooked picture — t i l t

Unscrambled word: _____ (antics)

Definition: _____ (wild or funny actions, often engaged in to get attention)

(Note: Definition may vary.)

Read the following selection to get the general meaning. Read it a second time, paying special attention to the words in dark type. Notice how they are used in sentences. These are Master Words. These are the words you will be working with in this lesson.

From **Cool Cat**
by Frank Bonham

At nine o'clock the next morning, Buddy sat in a deck chair before his home, gazing out over treetops and flat city blocks and **tingling** with **expectation**. In the house, he could hear Rich talking to Angie, his sister. Rich had just arrived on his motor scooter. Buddy's younger brother, Ralphie, was inside somewhere playing a music box. Buddy could hear the mindless **tinkle** of it going on steadily: "Four-and-twenty blackbirds . . ."

Buddy saw everything through an **opalescent haze** of hope, dreaming of those off-center bats of Cool's uncle's . . . just a **hunch**, that if they all let their minds stretch a little, they'd find some moneymaking plan to move them.

From where he sat, he could see a sweep of **multicolored** tar-paper roofs. Farther out rose little hills that were part of the area known as Dogtown. This area reached for miles, an **irregular** pattern of poor neighborhoods— black, brown, white, Oriental, mixed. In the distance, factories belched out gray toadstools of smoke.

Very close behind Buddy's house towered a range of high, brushy hills. The Williams home was on a narrow street that snaked along a steep hillside. It was built on the high side of the street, so that the earth had had to be **excavated** to make room for the garage. The house was built above the garage and was set back from its flat roof, which was graveled and railed to serve as a front yard. Redwood furniture and plants in wooden tubs stood under the porch eaves.

When an automobile horn mooed like a cow, Buddy **lurched** from the chair and went to the railing above the street.

EXERCISE 1

SELF-TEST: After reading the above selection, do the following. Look at the Master Words below. Underline the words that you think you know. Circle the words that you are less sure about. Draw a square around the words you don't recognize.

MASTER WORDS

excavate	**lurch**
expectation	**multicolored**
haze	**opalescent**
hunch	**tingle**
irregular	**tinkle**

Read the selection on the preceding page again, this time paying special attention to the ten Master Words. In the (a) spaces provided below, write down what you think is the meaning of the word. After you have attempted a definition for each word, look up the word in a dictionary. In the (b) spaces, copy the appropriate dictionary definition.

1. **excavate** (v.)

   a. _______________________________________

   b. to hollow out; to dig out

2. **expectation** (n.)

   a. _______________________________________

   b. an eager anticipation of an event

3. **haze** (n.)

   a. _______________________________________

   b. a clouded mental state; a slight fog, mist, or smoke in the air

4. **hunch** (n.)

   a. _______________________________________

   b. a strong feeling, often not based on facts, that something will happen

5. **irregular** (adj.)

   a. _______________________________________

   b. not conforming to an expected pattern; lacking evenness and balance

6. **lurch** (v.)

   a. _______________________________________

   b. to roll or sway suddenly

7. **multicolored** (adj.)

   a. _______________________________________

   b. consisting of many colors

8. **opalescent** (adj.)

   a. _______________________________________

   b. like a rainbow; reflecting an iridescent light

9. **tingle** (v.)

   a. _______________________________________

   b. to feel a stinging, prickling, or thrilling sensation

10. **tinkle** (n.)

   a. _______________________________________

   b. a short, light, ringing sound

Use the following list of synonyms and antonyms to fill in the blanks. Some words have no antonyms. In such cases, the antonym blanks have been marked with an X.

balanced	colorful	dig	hope	mist	sting
certainty	colorless	fill	jerk	monochrome	suspicion
clang	despair	glide	jingle	rainbow-colored	uneven
clear					

	Synonyms	**Antonyms**
1. **tingle**	(sting)	X
2. **expectation**	(hope)	(despair)
3. **tinkle**	(jingle)	(clang)
4. **opalescent**	(rainbow-colored) (colorful)	(colorless) (monochrome)
5. **haze**	(mist)	(clear)
6. **hunch**	(suspicion)	(certainty)
7. **multicolored**	(colorful) (rainbow-colored)	(monochrome) (colorless)
8. **irregular**	(uneven)	(balanced)
9. **excavate**	(dig)	(fill)
10. **lurch**	(jerk)	(glide)

Decide whether the first pair in the items below are synonyms or antonyms. Then choose the Master Word that shows a similar relation to the word(s) preceding the blank.

1. tilt	:tip	::stagger	:	(lurch)
2. crumple	:straighten	::single-hued	:	(multicolored)
3. applicant	:interviewee	::fog	:	(haze)
4. suspicion	:certainty	::orderly	:	(irregular)
5. prop	:reinforce	::eagerness	:	(expectation)
6. dutiful	:disobedient	::gong	:	(tinkle)
7. entirely	:fully	::guess	:	(hunch)
8. despair	:trust	::bury	:	(excavate)
9. maitre d'	:chief server	::shimmering	:	(opalescent)
10. mislead	:fool	::prickle	:	(tingle)

LESSON NINE

The Master Words in this lesson are repeated below. From the Master Words, choose the appropriate word for the blank in each of the following sentences. Write the word in the numbered space provided at the right.

excavate	haze	irregular	multicolored	tingle
expectation	hunch	lurch	opalescent	tinkle

1. While most of the flags in the world are ...?..., that island nation has a plain green banner.

1. _______ (multicolored)

2. Clothing that is flawed in some way is often marked "...?..." and sold at a lower price.

2. _______ (irregular)

3. The construction crew began to ...?... the area where the new shopping center was to be.

3. _______ (excavate)

4. The train's sudden stop caused everyone to ...?... forward.

4. _______ (lurch)

5. The children delighted in the brief ...?... splendor of the soap bubbles they were blowing.

5. _______ (opalescent)

6. The trees and buildings looked blurred and fuzzy in the early morning ...?... .

6. _______ (haze)

7. The ...?... of bells whenever the door opened told the shopkeeper that a customer had entered her shop.

7. _______ (tinkle)

8. Coach Bronson had great ...?...(s) for our team; he believed we could win the conference championship.

8. _______ (expectation)

9. Mary's cheek was numb as she left the dentist's office, but as the pain-killer wore off, her face began to ...?... .

9. _______ (tingle)

10. Jim had (a, an) ...?... he had taken a wrong turn when the houses became fewer and fewer.

10. _______ (hunch)

Order the words in each item from *least* to *most.* Use the abbreviations *L* for "least" and *M* for "most." Leave the line before the word of the middle degree blank. The first word provides a clue about how to arrange the words. See the example.

satisfied: __L__ pleased __M__ thrilled ____ delighted
(*Pleased* indicates the least satisfied; *thrilled* indicates the most satisfied.)

1. clumsy: ____ tumble __(M)__ crash __(L)__ lurch

2. colorful: ____ marbled __(M)__ opalescent __(L)__ faded

3. odd: ____ irregular __(L)__ normal __(M)__ weird

4. loud: ____ chime __(M)__ clang __(L)__ tinkle

5. overcast: __(M)__ pea soup ____ cloudy __(L)__ haze

6. sure: __(M)__ certainty __(L)__ hunch ____ probability

7. painful: ____ ache __(L)__ tingle __(M)__ torment

8. colorful: ____ tricolored __(L)__ single-hued __(M)__ multicolored

9. anticipation: __(L)__ mild interest __(M)__ yearning ____ expectation

10. digging: __(M)__ excavate __(L)__ scratch ____ furrow

(Note: In some cases, answers may vary.)

Read the following selection to get the general meaning. Read it a second time, paying special attention to the words in dark type. Notice how they are used in sentences. These are Master Words. These are the words you will be working with in this section.

from **Reason for Hope:**
A Spiritual Journey
by Jane Goodall with Phillip Berman

From the earliest years at Gombe I had been fascinated and delighted by the friendly and **nurturing** behavior that I observed so often among the **chimpanzees**. Peaceful **interactions** within a community are seen much more often than **aggressive** ones. Indeed, for hours, even days, one can follow a small group of chimps and see no aggression at all. Of course, these chimpanzees are, as we have seen, capable of violence and **brutality**. But fights between members of the same community **seldom** last more than a few seconds and rarely result in wounding. For the most part, relationships between the members of a community are relaxed and friendly, and we see frequent expressions of caring, helping, **compassion, altruism,** and most definitely a form of love.

Chimpanzees are **intensely** physical. When friends meet, after a separation, they may **embrace** and kiss each other. When they are fearful or suddenly terribly excited they reach out to touch each other—sometimes they show a whole orgy of contact-seeking behaviors, embracing, pressing open mouths upon each other, patting each other, holding hands.

EXERCISE 1

SELF-TEST: After reading the above selection, do the following. Look at the Master Words below. Underline the words that you think you know. Circle the words that you are less sure about. Draw a square around the words you don't recognize.

MASTER WORDS

aggressive	embrace
altruism	intensely
brutality	interactions
chimpanzees	nurturing
compassion	seldom

Read the selection on the preceding page again, this time paying special attention to the ten Master Words. In the (a) spaces provided below, write down what you think is the meaning of the word. After you have attempted a definition for each word, look up the word in a dictionary. In the (b) spaces, copy the appropriate dictionary definition.

1. **aggressive** (adj.)v

 a. ______________________________

 b. ___ marked by forceful energy

2. **altruism** (n.)

 a. ______________________________

 b. ___ philanthropy; unselfish action to benefit others

3. **brutality** (n.)

 a. ______________________________

 b. ___ cruel or beastly behavior

4. **chimpanzees** (n.)

 a. ______________________________

 b. ___ small African apes

5. **compassion** (n.)

 a. ______________________________

 b. ___ pity; sympathetic desire to help others

6. **embrace** (v.)

 a. ______________________________

 b. ___ touch with affection; hug

7. **intensely** (adv.)

 a. ______________________________

 b. ___ extremely

8. **interactions** (n.)

 a. ______________________________

 b. ___ mutual actions or influence

9. **nurturing** (adj.)

 a. ______________________________

 b. ___ nourishing; training

10. **seldom** (adv.)

 a. ______________________________

 b. ___ rarely

Use the following list of synonyms and antonyms to fill in the blanks. Some of the words have no antonyms. In such cases, the antonym blanks have been marked with an X.

associations forceful passive selfishness stifling
collaborations hug philanthropy slightly sympathy
cruelty nourishing rarely small apes tenderness
extremely often

	Synonyms	**Antonyms**
1. **nurturing**	(nourishing)	(stifling)
2. **chimpanzees**	(small apes)	X
3. **interactions**	(collaborations)	X
4. **aggressive**	(forceful)	(passive)
5. **brutality**	(cruelty)	(tenderness)
6. **seldom**	(rarely)	(often)
7. **compassion**	(sympathy)	(selfishness or cruelty)
8. **altruism**	(philanthropy)	(selfishness)
9. **intensely**	(extremely)	(slightly)
10. **embrace**	(hug)	X

Decide whether the first pair in the items below are synonyms or antonyms. Then choose the Master Word that shows a similar relation to the word(s) preceding the blank.

1. fame	:obscurity	::frequently	:	(seldom)
2. compete	:vie	::nourishing	:	(nurturing)
3. protest	:dissent	::associations	:	(interactions)
4. conceal	:hide	::extremely	:	(intensely)
5. immediate	:impending	::hug	:	(embrace)
6. obvious	:hidden	::cruelty	:	(compassion)
7. transcend	:rise above	::small apes	:	(chimpanzees)
8. reward	:punishment	::gentleness	:	(brutality)
9. breach	:gap	::philanthropy	:	(altruism)
10. gross	:refined	::passive	:	(aggressive)

The Master Words in this lesson are repeated below. From the Master Words, choose the appropriate word for the blank in each of the following sentences. Write the word in the numbered space provided at the right.

aggressive	brutality	compassion	intensely	nurturing
altruism	chimpanzees	embrace	interactions	seldom

1. The committee awarded the couple a humanitarian award for their acts of ...?... on behalf of the refugees.

1. _____ (altruism) _____

2. He had hoped for frequent letters, but instead he ...?... heard from her.

2. _____ (seldom) _____

3. When the child was found, her mother welcomed her with a tearful ...?... .

3. _____ (embrace) _____

4. The movie showed the utter ...?... both sides displayed during the war.

4. _____ (brutality) _____

5. The mother cat showed great affection to her kittens as she was ...?... them.

5. _____ (nurturing) _____

6. She loved the many animals at the zoo, but the ...?... playing in the trees were her favorites.

6. _____ (chimpanzees) _____

7. She hated pushy salespeople, and this one was the most ...?... she'd ever had to deal with.

7. _____ (aggressive) _____

8. At first they snarled, but then gradually their ...?... improved.

8. _____ (interactions) _____

9. The music touched them ...?... with feelings of both sorrow and joy.

9. _____ (intensely) _____

10. Acts of altruism are usually motivated by sincere ...?... for others.

10. _____ (compassion) _____

The invented words below are formed from parts of different Master Words from this lesson. Create a definition and indicate the part of speech for each word. The first one is done for you.

seldembrace   *(n.) a rare show of affection*

altruactions   (n. mutual influence that results in charitable donations)

brutensely   (adv. with extreme cruelty)

compaggressive   (adj. forcefully sympathetic)

Now invent your own words by combining parts of the Master Words. Create a definition for each, and indicate the word's part of speech. You may use any of the word parts above in new combinations.

Answers will vary.

____

____

____

Read the following selection to get the general meaning. Read it a second time, paying special attention to the words in dark type. Notice how they are used in sentences. These are Master Words. These are the words you will be working with in this lesson.

From **Five Little Peppers and How They Grew** by Margaret Sidney

The good times were coming for Polly—coming pretty near, and she didn't know it! All the children were in on the secret, for, as Mrs. Pepper declared, "They'd have to know it; and if they were let into the secret they'd keep it better."

So they had **individually** and **collectively** been entrusted with the precious secret and **charged** with the extreme importance of "never letting anyone know," and they had been nearly bursting ever since with the wild desire to [share] their knowledge.

"I'm afraid I *shall* tell," said David, running to his mother at last. "Oh, mammy, I don't dare stay near Polly, I do want to tell *so bad.*"

"Oh, no, you won't, David," said his mother encouragingly, "when you know mother [doesn't] want you to; and besides, think how Polly'll look when she sees it."

"I know," cried David, in the greatest **rapture**, "I wouldn't tell for all the world! I guess she'll look nice, don't you, mother?" and he laughed in **glee** at the thought.

"Poor child! I guess she will!" and then Mrs. Pepper laughed too, till the little old kitchen rang with delight at the **accustomed** sound.

The children all had to play "clap in and clap out" in the bedroom while *it* came; and "stagecoach" too. "Anything to make a noise," Ben said. And then after they got nicely started in the game, he would be missing to help about the mysterious thing in the kitchen, which was safe since Polly couldn't see him go on account of her bandage. So she didn't suspect in the least. And although the rest were almost dying to be out in the kitchen, they **conscientiously** stuck to their bargain to keep Polly occupied. Only Joel *would* open the door and **peep** once; and then Phronsie behind him began—"Oh, I see the sto—" but David **swooped** down on her in a twinkling and **smothered** the rest by tickling her.

EXERCISE 1

SELF-TEST: After reading the above selection, do the following. Look at the Master Words below. Underline the words that you think you know. Circle the words that you are less sure about. Draw a square around the words you don't recognize.

MASTER WORDS

accustomed	**individual**
charge	**peep**
collective	**rapture**
conscientious	**smother**
glee	**swoop**

LESSON ELEVEN

Read the selection on the preceding page again, this time paying special attention to the ten Master Words. In the (a) spaces provided below, write down what you think is the meaning of the word. After you have attempted a definition for each word, look up the word in a dictionary. In the (b) spaces, copy the appropriate dictionary definition.

1. **accustomed** (adj.)

    a. ____

    b. ___ customary; usual; habitual; familiar through use or repeated experience

2. **charge** (v.)

    a. ____

    b. ___ to trust with a responsibility or duty; to place a load or burden upon

3. **collective** (adj.)

    a. ____

    b. ___ having to do with a group of individuals viewed as a whole; mass; sum

4. **conscientious** (adj.)

    a. ____

    b. ___ controlled by one's conscience or one's sense of right; just; upright; careful

5. **glee** (n.)

    a. ____

    b. ___ joy; merriment; exultation; delight

6. **individual** (adj.)

    a. ____

    b. ___ involving or concerning a single person or thing; particular; separate

7. **peep** (v.)

    a. ____

    b. ___ to look at slyly or secretly, especially through a small opening

8. **rapture** (n.)

    a. ____

    b. ___ extreme joy or delight; ecstasy

9. **smother** (v.)

    a. ____

    b. ___ to hide by covering up; to suppress; to suffocate

10. **swoop** (v.)

    a. ____

    b. ___ to descend suddenly, often in an attack

Use the following list of synonyms and antonyms to fill in the blanks. Some words have no antonyms. In such cases, the antonym blanks have been marked with an X.

burden	despondence	joint	peek	separate	suppress
careful	dive	mirth	relieve	single	untypical
careless	encourage	overjoyfulness	rise	sorrow	usual
combined	gaze				

	Synonyms	**Antonyms**
1. **individual**	(separate) (single)	(joint) (combined)
2. **collective**	(combined) (joint)	(single) (separate)
3. **charge**	(burden)	(relieve)
4. **rapture**	(overjoyfulness)	(despondence) (sorrow)
5. **glee**	(mirth)	(sorrow) (despondence)
6. **accustomed**	(usual)	(untypical)
7. **conscientious**	(careful)	(careless)
8. **peep**	(peek)	(gaze)
9. **swoop**	(dive)	(rise)
10. **smother**	(suppress)	(encourage)

Decide whether the first pair in the items below are synonyms or antonyms. Then choose the Master Word that shows a similar relation to the word(s) preceding the blank.

1. porous	:watertight	::reckless	:	(conscientious)
2. vessel	:jar	::glance	:	(peep)
3. utter	:slight	::fan	:	(smother)
4. filter	:sieve	::tax	:	(charge)
5. nape	:scruff	::united	:	(collective)
6. vise	:clasp	::pounce	:	(swoop)
7. random	:orderly	::sadness	:	(glee)
8. veranda	:porch	::single	:	(individual)
9. compliment	:put-down	::unfamiliar	:	(accustomed)
10. brim	:rim	::joy	:	(rapture)

The Master Words in this lesson are repeated below. From the Master Words, choose the appropriate word for the blank in each of the following sentences. Write the word in the numbered space provided at the right.

| accustomed | collective | glee | peep | smother |
| charge | conscientious | individual | rapture | swoop |

1. The artist realized that he should not ...?... his creative ideas, no matter how wild those ideas seemed to be.

1. _______ (smother)

2. They tried to ...?... through the fence to watch the baseball game.

2. _______ (peep)

3. The caretaker was ...?...(d, ed) with the duty of keeping the museum safe and clean.

3. _______ (charge)

4. The South American condor, with a wing span of twelve feet, has been known to ...?... down upon a full-grown llama.

4. _______ (swoop)

5. Rodney's ...?... violin practice paid off when he was selected as a member of the youth orchestra.

5. _______ (conscientious)

6. The ...?... list of demands was compiled by both groups.

6. _______ (collective)

7. My little brother is a mischief-maker who laughs in ...?... whenever I fall for one of his practical jokes.

7. _______ (glee)

8. Having been born in the zoo, the young lions were not ...?... to hunting their own food.

8. _______ (accustomed)

9. Some students participate in sports; others, in music, drama, or science clubs, depending on their ...?... interests.

9. _______ (individual)

10. When they were reunited after thirty years, the loving sisters were in a state of ...?... .

10. _______ (rapture)

Write the Master Word that is associated with each word group below. Then list three things that might be associated with the review word that follows.

1. hardworking, dependable, trustworthy _______ (conscientious)

2. crack, spy hole, keyhole _______ (peep)

3. load, weigh down, saddle _______ (charge)

4. affection, kisses, pillow _______ (smother)

5. hang glider, flying squirrel, eagle _______ (swoop)

6. victory, party, merrymaking _______ (glee)

7. fingerprint, one-serving meal, solo flight _______ (individual)

8. family, herd, team _______ (collective)

9. usual comforts, status quo, habits _______ (accustomed)

10. bliss, ecstasy, cloud nine _______ (rapture)

Review word: gaze (Lesson 6)

_______ (birdwatchers) _______ (astronomers) _______ (daydreamers)

(Note: Answers may vary.)

Part I: From the list below, choose the appropriate word for each sentence that follows. Use each word only once. There will be two words left over.

affirm	collective	hunch	intent	oblige
brutality	disciplinarian	imprudent	irregular	rely
coincidence	distribute	individual	nurturing	

1. Sometimes students _____(distribute)_____ the tests, but only the teacher gathers them up.

2. Although the television was playing and there was much activity in the room, Margaret was _____(intent)_____ on her reading.

3. Though the mayor _____(affirm)_____ (d, ed) that she would cut the city budget, she did not keep her promise.

4. Many people think stockpiling nuclear weapons is _____(imprudent)_____ and dangerous.

5. Meeting our next-door neighbors by chance a thousand miles from home was indeed (a, an) _____(coincidence)_____.

6. My grandfather was a _____(nurturing)_____ character, taking care of all the children in the neighborhood.

7. The chances of changing policies are greater if we make (a, an) _____(collective)_____ protest than if we act separately.

8. We tend to think of animals as kind and gentle creatures, but sometimes their _____(brutality)_____ towards other animals can shock us.

9. The _____(irregular)_____ spread of the branches left our evergreen looking bare on one side.

10. Because the road was closed for repairs, we were _____(oblige)_____ (d, ed) to take a ten-mile detour.

11. The substitute teacher was a _____(disciplinarian)_____ and wouldn't allow for any misbehavior.

12. I buy from that store because I can _____(rely)_____ on their well-made products.

Part II: Decide whether the first pair in the items below are synonyms or antonyms. Then choose a Master Word from Lessons 1–11 that shows a similar relation to the word(s) preceding the blank. Do not repeat a Master Word that appears in the first column.

1. recognize	:acknowledge	::consciousness	:	(awareness)
2. filter	:blender	::occasional	:	(constant)
3. expectation	:anticipation	::cloudiness	:	(haze)
4. ration	:allowance	::bother	:	(irritate)
5. dutiful	:respectful	::familiar	:	(accustomed)

Part III: From the list below, choose the appropriate word for each sentence that follows. Use each word only once. There will be three words left over.

adventurous	assume	dignity	heritage	mechanical
antiseptic	attitude	duplication	immovable	philosophy
applicant	conscientious	excavate	ironical	relish

1. I _______ (assume) _______ that man lives nearby since he's always walking around the neighborhood, but I'm not sure.

2. Though she slipped on a banana peel and ended up rolling in mud, Chrissie was able to maintain her _______ (dignity) _______ in front of her classmates.

3. Winston was (a, an) _______ (conscientious) _______ worker who reported to work on time and did his best while he was on the job.

4. Lynn was _______ (adventurous) _______ and loved traveling to foreign countries.

5. Some household cleaners contain _______ (antiseptic) _______ agents that fight germs.

6. To compliment the cook on a meal that has been burned is being _______ (ironical) _______ .

7. Ralph was extremely discouraged when the manager told him that he was the fortieth _______ (applicant) _______ for the part-time position.

8. Though Marc declared that the health warning about smoking didn't scare him, his _______ (attitude) _______ changed when his father died of lung cancer.

9. Folding a paper on which a wet ink blot appears will result in the _______ (duplication) _______ of the pattern.

10. The builders brought in bulldozers to _______ (excavate) _______ the land and put in the basement of the house.

11. The Declaration of Independence and the Constitution are parts of our national _______ (heritage) _______ .

12. People particularly seem to _______ (relish) _______ ice cream on a hot summer day.

Part IV: Decide whether the first pair in the items below are synonyms or antonyms. Then choose a Master Word from Lessons 1–11 that shows a similar relation to the word(s) preceding the blank. Do not repeat a Master Word that appears in the first column.

1. obstacle :impediment ::warning : _______ (admonitions) _______

2. disengage :fasten ::carry on : _______ (hesitate) _______

3. rapture :elation ::hire : _______ (employ) _______

4. mislead :guide ::degrading : _______ (promoting) _______

5. expert :masterful ::eagerly : _______ (greedily) _______

Read the following selection to get the general meaning. Read it a second time, paying special attention to the words in dark type. Notice how they are used in sentences. These are Master Words. These are the words you will be working with in this lesson.

Adapted from **The Land of Oz**
by L. Frank Baum

The Scarecrow, with great politeness, introduced Tip and Jack Pumpkinhead, and the **latter personage** seemed to interest the Tin Woodman greatly.

"You are not very **substantial**, I must admit," said the Emperor; "but you are certainly unusual, and therefore worthy to become a member of our **select society**."

"I thank your Majesty," said Jack, **humbly**.

"I hope you are enjoying good health?" continued the Woodman.

"At present, yes," replied the Pumpkinhead, with a sigh; "but I am in constant terror of the day when I shall spoil."

"Nonsense!" said the Emperor—but in a kindly, **sympathetic** tone. "Do not, I beg of you, **dampen** today's sun with the showers of tomorrow. For before your head has time to spoil you can have it canned, and in that way it may be **preserved indefinitely**."

EXERCISE 1

SELF-TEST: After reading the above selection, do the following. Look at the Master Words below. Underline the words that you think you know. Circle the words that you are less sure about. Draw a square around the words you don't recognize.

MASTER WORDS

dampen	**preserve**
humble	**select**
indefinite	**society**
latter	**substantial**
personage	**sympathetic**

Read the selection on the preceding page again, this time paying special attention to the ten Master Words. In the (a) spaces provided below, write down what you think is the meaning of the word. After you have attempted a definition for each word, look up the word in a dictionary. In the (b) spaces, copy the appropriate dictionary definition.

1. **dampen** (v.)

   a. ____

   b. to depress, discourage, or deaden; also, to moisten

2. **humble** (adj.)

   a. ____

   b. without pride or vanity; modest; meek; lowly

3. **indefinite** (adj.)

   a. ____

   b. not clearly defined or with no set limits

4. **latter** (adj.)

   a. ____

   b. being the second of two things mentioned

5. **personage** (n.)

   a. ____

   b. a person, especially one who is important or noteworthy

6. **preserve** (v.)

   a. ____

   b. to keep safe from injury, destruction, or decay

7. **select** (adj.)

   a. ____

   b. of special value or excellence; choice

8. **society** (n.)

   a. ____

   b. a group of persons linked for any reason, having common traditions and interests or ends

9. **substantial** (adj.)

   a. ____

   b. having body; solid; strong; firm

10. **sympathetic** (adj.)

   a. ____

   b. having feelings of compassion or understanding

Use the following list of synonyms and antonyms to fill in the blanks. Some words have no antonyms. In such cases, the antonym blanks have been marked with an X.

choice	dignitary	former	limited	save	solid
commoner	discourage	individual	organization	second	understanding
critical	encourage	inferior	proud	shy	unmeasured
destroy	flimsy				

	Synonyms	**Antonyms**
1. **latter**	(second)	(former)
2. **personage**	(dignitary)	(commoner)
3. **substantial**	(solid)	(flimsy)
4. **select**	(choice)	(inferior)
5. **society**	(organization)	(individual)
6. **humble**	(shy)	(proud)
7. **sympathetic**	(understanding)	(critical)
8. **dampen**	(discourage)	(encourage)
9. **preserve**	(save)	(destroy)
10. **indefinite**	(unmeasured)	(limited)

Decide whether the first pair in the items below are synonyms or antonyms. Then choose the Master Word that shows a similar relation to the word(s) preceding the blank.

1. conscientious	:irresponsible	::motivate	:	(dampen)
2. peep	:peek	::first-rate	:	(select)
3. charge	:trust	::club	:	(society)
4. smother	:stir up	::ruin	:	(preserve)
5. glee	:gloom	::previous	:	(latter)
6. collective	:joint	::strong	:	(substantial)
7. swoop	:descend	::celebrity	:	(personage)
8. accustomed	:new	::boastful	:	(humble)
9. individual	:group	::uncaring	:	(sympathetic)
10. rapture	:delight	::limitless	:	(indefinite)

The Master Words in this lesson are repeated below. From the Master Words, choose the appropriate word for the blank in each of the following sentences. Write the word in the numbered space provided at the right.

dampen	indefinite	personage	select	substantial
humble	latter	preserve	society	sympathetic

1. President Lincoln was determined to ...?... the Union.

   1. ________________ (preserve)

2. Toby's opponent had nearly pinned him, but that did not ...?... his hopes of winning the wrestling match.

   2. ________________ (dampen)

3. None of the prisoners knew when they would be released because they all had been given ...?... sentences.

   3. ________________ (indefinite)

4. ...?...(s) from around the world came to the funeral to mourn the President's death.

   4. ________________ (Personage)

5. Only ...?... students were accepted as members of the Honor Society.

   5. ________________ (select)

6. Although the police believed Jenkins was the thief, they could find no ...?... evidence to support their suspicion.

   6. ________________ (substantial)

7. The Chamber of Commerce is (a, an) ...?... of businesspeople who work in the collective interest of the community.

   7. ________________ (society)

8. I enjoy baseball and football, but I prefer the ...?... because I once was a halfback.

   8. ________________ (latter)

9. Brian was extremely ...?... as he accepted the medal of heroism, saying that anyone else would have acted as he had.

   9. ________________ (humble)

10. A good friend knows when to give advice and when to just lend (a, an) ...?... ear.

   10. ________________ (sympathetic)

Fill in the chart below with the Master Word that fits each set of clues. Part of speech refers to the word's usage in the lesson. Use a dictionary when necessary.

Number of Syllables	Part of Speech	Other Clues		Master Word
3	noun	a VIP is also this	1.	(personage)
4	adjective	*apathetic* is its opposite	2.	(sympathetic)
4	adjective	the number of stars in the sky is this	3.	(indefinite)
2	adjective	the chosen few	4.	(select)
4	noun	a loner does not care for this	5.	(society)
2	verb	to make a pickle, you have to do this	6.	(preserve)
2	verb	"lay a wet blanket on"	7.	(dampen)
2	adjective	*arrogant* is its opposite	8.	(humble)
2	adjective	last-mentioned	9.	(latter)
3	adjective	no small thing	10.	(substantial)

Read the following selection to get the general meaning. Read it a second time, paying special attention to the words in dark type. Notice how they are used in sentences. These are Master Words. These are the words you will be working with in this lesson.

From **Around the World in Eighty Days**
by Jules Verne

As for Passepartout, he was a true Parisian of Paris. Since he had **abandoned** his own country for England, taking service as a **valet**, he had in vain searched for a master after his own heart. Passepartout was by no means one of these **pert dunces depicted** by Moliere, with a bold gaze and a nose held high in the air; he was an honest fellow, with a pleasant face, lips a **trifle protruding**, soft-mannered and **serviceable**, with a good round head, such as one likes to see on the shoulders of a friend. His eyes were blue, his complexion **rubicund**, his figure almost **portly** and well built, his body muscular, and his physical powers fully developed by the exercises of his younger days. His brown hair was somewhat tumbled; for while the ancient sculptors are said to have known eighteen methods of arranging Minerva's tresses, Passepartout was familiar with but one of dressing his own: three strokes of a large-tooth comb completed his [grooming].

EXERCISE 1

SELF-TEST: After reading the above selection, do the following. Look at the Master Words below. Underline the words that you think you know. Circle the words that you are less sure about. Draw a square around the words you don't recognize.

MASTER WORDS

abandon	**protrude**
depict	**rubicund**
dunce	**serviceable**
pert	**trifle**
portly	**valet**

Read the selection on the preceding page again, this time paying special attention to the ten Master Words. In the (a) spaces provided below, write down what you think is the meaning of the word. After you have attempted a definition for each word, look up the word in a dictionary. In the (b) spaces, copy the appropriate dictionary definition.

1. **abandon** (v.)

   a. _______________________________

   b. _____ to leave, especially completely and forever; to forsake

2. **depict** (v.)

   a. _______________________________

   b. _____ to give a picture of, often by use of words; to portray; to describe

3. **dunce** (n.)

   a. _______________________________

   b. _____ a dull-witted or stupid person

4. **pert** (adj.)

   a. _______________________________

   b. _____ bold; forward; lively; sassy

5. **portly** (adj.)

   a. _______________________________

   b. _____ large in body; stout

6. **protrude** (v.)

   a. _______________________________

   b. _____ to stick out; to project

7. **rubicund** (adj.)

   a. _______________________________

   b. _____ reddish or ruddy in complexion

8. **serviceable** (adj.)

   a. _______________________________

   b. _____ fit for performing a duty; useful

9. **trifle** (n.)

   a. _______________________________

   b. _____ a little bit; a matter of small importance or value

10. **valet** (n.)

   a. _______________________________

   b. _____ a servant or attendant who takes care of the clothing and grooming of an employer or customers

Use the following list of synonyms and antonyms to fill in the blanks. Some words have no antonyms. In such cases, the antonym blanks have been marked with an X.

bit	genius	pale	reddish	servant	timid
describe	master	project	remain	slim	useful
desert	misrepresent	recede	sassy	stout	useless
fool	much				

	Synonyms	**Antonyms**
1. **abandon**	(desert)	(remain)
2. **valet**	(servant)	(master)
3. **pert**	(sassy)	(timid)
4. **dunce**	(fool)	(genius)
5. **depict**	(describe)	(misrepresent)
6. **trifle**	(bit)	(much)
7. **protrude**	(project)	(recede)
8. **serviceable**	(useful)	(useless)
9. **rubicund**	(reddish)	(pale)
10. **portly**	(stout)	(slim)

Decide whether the first pair in the items below are synonyms or antonyms. Then choose the Master Word that shows a similar relation to the word(s) preceding the blank.

1. dampen	:hearten	::plenty	: (trifle)
2. select	:chosen	::handy	: (serviceable)
3. society	:community	::leave	: (abandon)
4. substantial	:sturdy	::picture	: (depict)
5. personage	:public figure	::rude	: (pert)
6. preserve	:protect	::simpleton	: (dunce)
7. latter	:first	::dent	: (protrude)
8. humble	:conceited	::thin	: (portly)
9. sympathetic	:unfeeling	::employer	: (valet)
10. indefinite	:unclear	::rosy	: (rubicund)

LESSON FOURTEEN

The Master Words in this lesson are repeated below. From the Master Words, choose the appropriate word for the blank in each of the following sentences. Write the word in the numbered space provided at the right.

abandon	dunce	portly	rubicund	trifle
depict	pert	protrude	serviceable	valet

1. Outdoor life gave many of the pioneers (a, an) ...?... complexion.

2. Polly was pleased to learn that the tiny glass animals she had admired cost only (a, an) ...?... .

3. The ...?... man waddled toward the chocolate bar.

4. Mark Twain vividly ...?...(d, ed) boyhood life along the Mississippi River in many of his stories and books.

5. When Elaine spilled sauce on her jacket, she gave it to the hotel ...?... to clean.

6. In a compound fracture, a broken bone may ...?... through the skin.

7. Everyone believed that Jack was able to do good work; no one could understand why he pretended to be a ...?... .

8. The ...?... child did not hesitate to tell the hostess that the meat was tough and the vegetables too salty.

9. The old sea captain refused to ...?... his ship, even when it was obvious that the vessel was sinking.

10. My ...?... car may not be sporty, but it always starts in the winter.

1. _______ (rubicund)

2. _______ (trifle)

3. _______ (portly)

4. _______ (depict)

5. _______ (valet)

6. _______ (protrude)

7. _______ (dunce)

8. _______ (pert)

9. _______ (abandon)

10. _______ (serviceable)

To complete the word spiral, choose the Master Word associated with each phrase below. Start with 1 and fill in each answer clockwise. Be careful! Each new word may overlap the previous word by one or more letters.

1. personal attendant

2. just a smidgen

3. after jogging, your face may look like this

4. a slow-witted person might be called this

5. leave behind for good

6. smart-alecky

7. radios and blow-dryers are this

8. noses and ski jumps do this

9. paint a picture or describe

10. a hefty person is this

1. V	A	L	E	2. T	R	I	F
O	N	6. P	E	R	T	7. S	L
D	T	R	U	9. D	E	E	E
N	O	T	L	Y	P	R	3. R
A	R	R			I	V	U
B	8. P	O	10. P	T	C	I	B
5. A	E	L	B	A	E	C	I
E	C	N	U	4. D	N	U	C

Read the following selection to get the general meaning. Read it a second time, paying special attention to the words in dark type. Notice how they are used in sentences. These are Master Words. These are the words you will be working with in this lesson.

Adapted from **Black Beauty**
by Anna Sewell

I went on the stand at eight in the morning, and had done a good share of work, when we had to take a fare to the railway. A long train was just expected in, so my driver pulled up at the back of some of the outside cabs to take the chance of a return fare. It was a very heavy train, and as all the cabs were soon **engaged** ours was called for. There was a party of four; a noisy, **blustery** man with a lady, a little boy and a young girl, and a great deal of luggage. The lady and the boy got into the cab, and while the man ordered about the luggage the young girl came and looked at me.

"Papa," she said, "I am sure this poor horse cannot take us and all our luggage so far, he is so very weak and worn out. Do look at him."

"Oh! he's all right, miss," said my driver, "he's strong enough."

"Papa, papa, do take a second cab," said the young girl in a **beseeching** tone. "I am sure we are wrong, I am sure it is very cruel."

"Nonsense, Grace, get in at once, and don't make all this fuss."

My gentle friend had to obey, and box after box was dragged up and **lodged** on the top of the cab or settled by the side of the driver. At last all was ready, and with his usual jerk at the rein and **slash** of the whip he drove out of the station.

The load was very heavy and I had had neither food nor rest since morning; but I did my best, as I always had done, in spite of cruelty and **injustice**.

I got along fairly till we came to Ludgate Hill, but there the heavy load and my own **exhaustion** were too much. I was struggling to keep on, **goaded** by constant **chucks** of the rein and use of the whip, when in a single moment—I cannot tell how—my feet slipped from under me, and I fell heavily to the ground on my side; the suddenness and the force with which I fell seemed to beat all the breath out of my body. I thought I heard that sweet, **pitiful** voice saying, "Oh! that poor horse! It is all our fault."

EXERCISE 1

SELF-TEST: After reading the above selection, do the following. Look at the Master Words below. Underline the words that you think you know. Circle the words that you are less sure about. Draw a square around the words you don't recognize.

MASTER WORDS

beseech	goad
blustery	injustice
chuck	lodge
engaged	pitiful
exhaustion	slash

Read the selection on the preceding page again, this time paying special attention to the ten Master Words. In the (a) spaces provided below, write down what you think is the meaning of the word. After you have attempted a definition for each word, look up the word in a dictionary. In the (b) spaces, copy the appropriate dictionary definition.

1. **beseech** (v.)

   a. ____

   b. _____ to beg, implore, appeal, or plead

2. **blustery** (adj.)

   a. ____

   b. _____ roaring, violent, as a strong wind or an angry person, often making empty threats; boisterous

3. **chuck** (n.)

   a. ____

   b. _____ a light tap or pat, especially under the chin

4. **engaged** (adj.)

   a. ____

   b. _____ busy; occupied; involved

5. **exhaustion** (n.)

   a. ____

   b. _____ extreme weakness, fatigue, or weariness

6. **goad** (v.)

   a. ____

   b. _____ to spur on or urge on; to stimulate

7. **injustice** (n.)

   a. ____

   b. _____ unjust or unfair treatment or deed; wrong

8. **lodge** (v.)

   a. ____

   b. _____ to place firmly in a particular position; to embed

9. **pitiful** (adj.)

   a. ____

   b. _____ deserving of compassion, sympathy, or pity

10. **slash** (n.)

   a. ____

   b. _____ a sweeping, cutting motion

Use the following list of synonyms and antonyms to fill in the blanks. Some words have no antonyms. In such cases, the antonym blanks have been marked with an X.

available	enviable	pathetic	quiet	right	tap
cut	grant	pep	remove	spur	unfairness
embed	occupied	plead	restrain	stormy	weariness

	Synonyms	**Antonyms**
1. **engaged**	(occupied)	(available)
2. **blustery**	(stormy)	(quiet)
3. **beseech**	(plead)	(grant)
4. **lodge**	(embed)	(remove)
5. **slash**	(cut)	X
6. **injustice**	(unfairness)	(right)
7. **exhaustion**	(weariness)	(pep)
8. **goad**	(spur)	(restrain)
9. **chuck**	(tap)	X
10. **pitiful**	(pathetic)	(enviable)

Decide whether the first pair in the items below are synonyms or antonyms. Then choose the Master Word that shows a similar relation to the word(s) preceding the blank.

1. trifle	:sizable	::give	: (beseech)
2. serviceable	:helpful	::pat	: (chuck)
3. dunce	:scholar	::energy	: (exhaustion)
4. abandon	:depart	::place	: (lodge)
5. protrude	:indent	::calm	: (blustery)
6. depict	:represent	::wrong	: (injustice)
7. pert	:outspoken	::stroke	: (slash)
8. portly	:slender	::free	: (engaged)
9. valet	:attendant	::heartbreaking	: (pitiful)
10. rubicund	:reddish	::urge	: (goad)

LESSON FIFTEEN

The Master Words in this lesson are repeated below. From the Master Words, choose the appropriate word for the blank in each of the following sentences. Write the word in the numbered space provided at the right.

beseech	chuck	exhaustion	injustice	pitiful
blustery	engaged	goad	lodge	slash

1. Some people believe that a great ...?... was done to the American Indians and that the government should right the old wrongs.

1. _______ (injustice) _______

2. Fred was ...?...(d, ed) into taking the dare against his better judgment.

2. _______ (goad) _______

3. Most young animals enjoy a playful ...?... under the chin.

3. _______ (chuck) _______

4. After searching all over the yard for the lost Frisbee, we finally found it ...?...(d, ed) in the apple tree.

4. _______ (lodge) _______

5. Mark was accustomed to running a mile every day, but after the five-mile race, he was overcome with ...?... .

5. _______ (exhaustion) _______

6. The prisoner wept and ...?...(d, ed) the queen to believe his story, but she refused to hear his plea.

6. _______ (beseech) _______

7. Mr. Kramer is (a, an) ...?... man who often scolds his class in a loud voice but rarely carries out his threats.

7. _______ (blustery) _______

8. We couldn't meet in the library because it was already ...?... .

8. _______ (engaged) _______

9. The ...?... face of the lost dog touched Mother's heart, and she gave him a few scraps of meat.

9. _______ (pitiful) _______

10. Daniel Boone ...?...(d, ed) a trail through the unexplored wilderness of Kentucky.

10. _______ (slash) _______

The invented words below are formed from parts of different Master Words from this lesson. Create a definition and indicate the part of speech for each word. The first one is done for you.

engagoad	*(v.) to push someone to become more involved*
goadchuck	([n.] a light pat under the chin intended to provoke another)
blusterseech	([v.] to beg violently or angrily)
slashaustion	([n.] fatigue brought on by use of a machete)

Now invent your own words by combining parts of the Master Words. Create a definition for each, and indicate the word's part of speech. (You may reuse any of the word parts above in new combinations.)

1. _______________   _____________________________

2. _______________   _____________________________

(Note: Answers will vary.)

Other possibilities:
goadseech   (v.) to beg or plead persuasively
pitiseech   (v.) to beg in a heartbreaking manner
slashlodge   (v.) to embed a blade (as of a knife or machete) into something

Read the following selection to get the general meaning. Read it a second time, paying special attention to the words in dark type. Notice how they are used in sentences. These are Master Words. These are the words you will be working with in this lesson.

From **The Log of a Cowboy**
by Andy Adams

We held the wagon and saddle horses in the rear, and when we were half a mile away from the trail **ford**, cut off about two hundred head of the leaders and started for the crossing, leaving only the horse **wrangler** and one man with the herd. On reaching the river we gave them an extra push, and the cattle **plunged** into the muddy water. Before the cattle had advanced fifty feet, **instinct** warned them of the **treacherous** footing, and the leaders tried to turn back; but by that time we had the entire bunch in the water and were urging them forward. They had halted but a moment and begun **milling**, when several heavy steers sank; then we gave way and allowed the rest to come back. We did not realize fully the treachery of this river until we saw that twenty cattle were caught in the **merciless** grasp of the quicksand. They sank slowly to the level of their bodies, which gave sufficient **resistance** to support their weight, but they were hopelessly **bogged**. We allowed the free cattle to return to the herd, and immediately turned our attention to those that were bogged, some of whom were nearly **submerged** by water.

EXERCISE 1

SELF-TEST: After reading the above selection, do the following. Look at the Master Words below. Underline the words that you think you know. Circle the words that you are less sure about. Draw a square around the words you don't recognize.

MASTER WORDS

bogged	**plunge**
ford	**resistance**
instinct	**submerge**
merciless	**treacherous**
mill	**wrangler**

Read the selection on the preceding page again, this time paying special attention to the ten Master Words. In the (a) spaces provided below, write down what you think is the meaning of the word. After you have attempted a definition for each word, look up the word in a dictionary. In the (b) spaces, copy the appropriate dictionary definition.

1. **bogged** (v.)

   a. _______________________________

   b. _____ to be sunk, as in wet, spongy ground

2. **ford** (n.)

   a. _______________________________

   b. _____ a place where a body of water may be crossed by wading

3. **instinct** (n.)

   a. _______________________________

   b. _____ a natural impulse, especially in animals, which leads them to act without conscious thought; unlearned behavior

4. **merciless** (adj.)

   a. _______________________________

   b. _____ lacking compassion or forgiveness; cruel; harsh

5. **mill** (v.)

   a. _______________________________

   b. _____ to move around in a confused or disorderly way

6. **plunge** (v.)

   a. _______________________________

   b. _____ to dive or thrust forcibly or suddenly, especially into a liquid

7. **resistance** (n.)

   a. _______________________________

   b. _____ a force that opposes or slows down a body or another force

8. **submerge** (v.)

   a. _______________________________

   b. _____ to cover, as by water

9. **treacherous** (adj.)

   a. _______________________________

   b. _____ not dependable; not to be trusted; deceptive; unreliable

10. **wrangler** (n.)

   a. _______________________________

   b. _____ one who herds cows or horses

Use the following list of synonyms and antonyms to fill in the blanks. Some words have no antonyms. In such cases, the antonym blanks have been marked with an X.

churn	cruel	dunk	kind	released	swamped
cowboy	dependable	emerge	learning	rise	unreliable
crossing	dive	impulse	opposition	submission	

	Synonyms	**Antonyms**
1. **ford**	(crossing)	X
2. **wrangler**	(cowboy)	X
3. **plunge**	(dive) (dunk)	(rise)
4. **instinct**	(impulse)	(learning)
5. **treacherous**	(unreliable)	(dependable)
6. **mill**	(churn)	X
7. **merciless**	(cruel)	(kind)
8. **resistance**	(opposition)	(submission)
9. **bogged**	(swamped)	(released)
10. **submerge**	(dunk) (dive)	(emerge)

Decide whether the first pair in the items below are synonyms or antonyms. Then choose the Master Word that shows a similar relation to the word(s) preceding the blank.

1. beseech	:command	::forgiving	: (merciless)
2. exhaustion	:liveliness	::loosed	: (bogged)
3. chuck	:poke	::sink	: (submerge)
4. blustery	:cool-headed	::training	: (instinct)
5. lodge	:plant	::circle	: (mill)
6. engaged	:unattached	::surface	: (plunge)
7. injustice	:mistreatment	::ranch hand	: (wrangler)
8. slash	:slice	::obstacle	: (resistance)
9. pitiful	:desirable	::safe	: (treacherous)
10. goad	:prod	::water passage	: (ford)

The Master Words in this lesson are repeated below. From the Master Words, choose the appropriate word for the blank in each of the following sentences. Write the word in the numbered space provided at the right.

bogged	instinct	mill	resistance	treacherous
ford	merciless	plunge	submerge	wrangler

1. We found a shallow place in the river that would serve as (a, an) ...?... where we could cross.

   1. _________ (ford) _________

2. Hans feared he would become stuck in the swamp because the ground offered no ...?... .

   2. _________ (resistance) _________

3. Although the walrus is not a fish but a mammal, it is able to remain ...?...(d, ed) for about twenty minutes.

   3. _________ (submerge) _________

4. For about an hour the young people declined to dance and just ...?...(d, ed) around the dance floor.

   4. _________ (mill) _________

5. The ...?... ruler put even innocent babies to death.

   5. _________ (merciless) _________

6. It is (a, an) ...?... of spiders to build webs.

   6. _________ (instinct) _________

7. When we pulled to the side of the road during the flash flood, our tires became ...?... in the soft shoulder.

   7. _________ (bogged) _________

8. One of the most exciting events in the life of a Texas ...?... was the long drive north on the Chisholm Trail.

   8. _________ (wrangler) _________

9. Suddenly the ...?... ice gave way, plunging us waist-deep into the water.

   9. _________ (treacherous) _________

10. The penguin waddled to the water's edge, then ...?...(d, ed) head-first to the bottom of the tank.

    10. _________ (plunge) _________

Order the words in each item from *least* to *most.* Use the abbreviations *L* for "least" and *M* for "most." Leave the line before the word of the middle degree blank. The first word provides a clue about how to arrange the words. See the example.

uncomfortable: _____pained __M__miserable __L__uneasy

(*Uneasy* indicates the least uncomfortable; *miserable* indicates the most uncomfortable.)

1. cruel: _____mean __(L)__pert __(M)__merciless

2. changeable: _____stability __(M)__flexibility __(L)__resistance

3. blocked: __(M)__bogged __(L)__slowed _____hindered

4. tightly packed: __(M)__crush _____crowd __(L)__mill

5. training: __(M)__drilling __(L)__instinct _____guidance

6. wet: _____dip __(L)__sprinkle __(M)__submerge

7. immersed: __(M)__plunge _____dip __(L)__float

8. elevated: _____low-water bridge __(L)__ford __(M)__overpass

9. authority: _____wrangler __(L)__groom __(M)__ranch owner

10. dangerous: __(M)__treacherous __(L)__questionable _____tricky

(Note: In some cases, answers may vary.)

Read the following selection to get the general meaning. Read it a second time, paying special attention to the words in dark type. Notice how they are used in sentences. These are Master Words. These are the words you will be working with in this lesson.

Adapted from **"The Happy Prince"**
by Oscar Wilde

High above the city, on a tall **pedestal**, stood the statue of the Happy Prince. He was **gilded** all over with thin leaves of fine gold; for eyes he had two bright **sapphires**, and a large red ruby glowed on his sword-hilt.

He was very much admired indeed. "He is as beautiful as a [weathervane]," remarked one of the Town **Councilors** who wished to gain a **reputation** for having artistic tastes; "only not quite so useful," he added, fearing that people should think him **impractical**, which he really was not.

"Why can't you be like the Happy Prince?" asked a **sensible** mother of her little boy who was crying for the Moon. "The Happy Prince never dreams of crying for anything."

"I am glad there is someone in the world who is quite happy," **muttered** a disappointed man as he gazed at the wonderful statue.

"He looks just like an angel," said the Charity Children as they came out of the cathedral in their bright scarlet **cloaks** and their clean white pinafores.

"How do you know?" said the Mathematical Master. "You have never seen one."

"Ah! but we have, in our dreams," answered the children; and the Mathematical Master frowned and looked very **severe**, for he did not approve of children dreaming.

EXERCISE 1

SELF-TEST: After reading the above selection, do the following. Look at the Master Words below. Underline the words that you think you know. Circle the words that you are less sure about. Draw a square around the words you don't recognize.

<table>
<tr><td colspan="2" align="center">MASTER WORDS</td></tr>
<tr><td>cloak</td><td>pedestal</td></tr>
<tr><td>councilor</td><td>reputation</td></tr>
<tr><td>gilded</td><td>sapphire</td></tr>
<tr><td>impractical</td><td>sensible</td></tr>
<tr><td>mutter</td><td>severe</td></tr>
</table>

Read the selection on the preceding page again, this time paying special attention to the ten Master Words. In the (a) spaces provided below, write down what you think is the meaning of the word. After you have attempted a definition for each word, look up the word in a dictionary. In the (b) spaces, copy the appropriate dictionary definition.

1. **cloak** (n.)

   a. ____

   b. _____ a loose outer garment, usually without sleeves; cape

2. **councilor** (n.)

   a. ____

   b. _____ a member of a group that makes laws, gives advice, or manages government

3. **gilded** (adj.)

   a. ____

   b. _____ coated with a thin layer of gold

4. **impractical** (adj.)

   a. ____

   b. _____ unrealistic or idealistic

5. **mutter** (v.)

   a. ____

   b. _____ to speak unclearly or in a low tone, often complaining

6. **pedestal** (n.)

   a. ____

   b. _____ a base or support, especially of a statue or pillar

7. **reputation** (n.)

   a. ____

   b. _____ the opinion held of a person by others, sometimes different from the person's real character

8. **sapphire** (n.)

   a. ____

   b. _____ a precious gem deep blue in color

9. **sensible** (adj.)

   a. ____

   b. _____ having common sense or good judgment; intelligent; reasonable

10. **severe** (adj.)

   a. ____

   b. _____ strict; stern; harsh

Use the following list of synonyms and antonyms to fill in the blanks. Some words have no antonyms. In such cases, the antonym blanks have been marked with an X.

anonymity   cape   gentle   official   top
base   fame   gold-coated   reasonable   unrealistic
blue gem   foolish   grumble   stern   wise

	Synonyms	**Antonyms**
1. **pedestal**	(base)	(top)
2. **gilded**	(gold-coated)	X
3. **sapphire**	(blue gem)	X
4. **councilor**	(official)	X
5. **reputation**	(fame)	(anonymity)
6. **impractical**	(unrealistic) (foolish)	(reasonable) (wise)
7. **sensible**	(wise) (reasonable)	(foolish) (unrealistic)
8. **mutter**	(grumble)	X
9. **cloak**	(cape)	X
10. **severe**	(stern)	(gentle)

Decide whether the first pair in the items below are synonyms or antonyms. Then choose the Master Word that shows a similar relation to the word(s) preceding the blank.

1. merciless	:understanding	::head	: (pedestal)
2. submerge	:immerse	::robe	: (cloak)
3. mill	:wander	::murmur	: (mutter)
4. wrangler	:herder	::blue gem	: (sapphire)
5. bogged	:freed	::down-to-earth	: (impractical)
6. resistance	:barrier	::gold-plated	: (gilded)
7. instinct	:instruction	::kind	: (severe)
8. ford	:pass	::name	: (reputation)
9. plunge	:float	::unwise	: (sensible)
10. treacherous	:deceptive	::representative	: (councilor)

The Master Words in this lesson are repeated below. From the Master Words, choose the appropriate word for the blank in each of the following sentences. Write the word in the numbered space provided at the right.

| cloak | gilded | mutter | reputation | sensible |
| councilor | impractical | pedestal | sapphire | severe |

1. The light weight of the statue clued Marissa that it was not solid gold, just ...?... .

   1. ______ (gilded) ______

2. Some colleges have a fine ...?... that they have not lived up to for many years.

   2. ______ (reputation) ______

3. The class had many ideas for money-making projects, but unfortunately they were all ...?... .

   3. ______ (impractical) ______

4. In most Hollywood versions of *Dracula*, the count wears a cape or (a, an) ...?... .

   4. ______ (cloak) ______

5. Michigan winters, with their snow, ice, and bitter cold, are very ...?... .

   5. ______ (severe) ______

6. Many of the town ...?...(s) believed the community's sewer system needed repairs.

   6. ______ (councilor) ______

7. The statue of General Grant on horseback was mounted on a six-foot ...?... .

   7. ______ (pedestal) ______

8. When wished a merry Christmas, Ebenezer Scrooge was known to ...?..., "Bah! Humbug!"

   8. ______ (mutter) ______

9. The setting of the ring included a deep-blue ...?... .

   9. ______ (sapphire) ______

10. Benjamin Franklin's *Poor Richard's Almanac* offers some ...?..., practical guidelines for living.

   10. ______ (sensible) ______

Use at least five Master Words from this lesson to write a scene about one of the following topics. Or create a topic of your own. Write your choice on the blank. Circle the Master Words as you use them.

Possible Topics: Mishap at the Museum, Field Trip Mix-up

____

____

____

____

____

____

____

(Note: Answers will vary.)

Read the following selection to get the general meaning. Read it a second time, paying special attention to the words in dark type. Notice how they are used in sentences. These are Master Words. These are the words you will be working with in this lesson.

From "**First Jump**"
by Henry Gregor Felsen

Ab got up. The plane was almost empty now. Only those who hadn't dared make the jump were still on board. Ab walked back and stood by the open hatch. He nodded mechanically as he heard the last instructions.

"Jump."

Ab took a deep breath. He wanted to step back, to run back to his seat. Far below him the world was turning slowly. It was so far away—so very far. He **clenched** his fists and dove out head first.

He was dropping. The wind rushed by, tearing at his nostrils. He tried to breathe, but couldn't. He was turning over and over. Above him he caught a brief **glimpse** of the transport, circling lazily around. Then he turned to see the ground rushing up at him.

He would have **yowled** in terror if he had had any breath to yowl with. He was dropping—dropping—

He remembered he had forgotten to count as he fell. What matter. Grasping **desperately**, he fought to find his ripcord. His fingernails tore against the flying suit as he clawed for it. Then his fingers closed around the metal ring and he pulled with all his strength.

It wasn't going to open! He was still falling, twisting, turning, **hurtling** toward the earth.

He **scrambled** madly to find the ripcord for his **reserve** pack. He couldn't find it. His twisting body was dropping so fast it almost whistled as it fell. He **flailed** around in despair as he prepared to smash into the ground.

Suddenly he was snapped upright. He looked up. The **chute** was spread wide, cutting his rate of **descent**. He was swinging and falling slowly.

Ab almost cried with relief. He pulled at his lines to drift toward the field. He was calm now, and enjoyed the feeling of dropping slowly. His heart was getting back to normal.

It took him a long time to get down, and finally he hit the smooth ground of the field, rolling over as he was pulled on by his chute. Ab scrambled to his feet and pulled the lines of his chute to spill the wind out of it. Then he gathered up the folds in his arms and walked toward the hangar.

They came out to meet him with a small truck. The driver laughed. "O.K., kid, you're down now."

"Huh?"

"You can let go of that ripcord ring," the driver laughed. "You won't need a chute to get off the truck."

EXERCISE 1

SELF-TEST: After reading the above selection, do the following. Look at the Master Words below. Underline the words that you think you know. Circle the words that you are less sure about. Draw a square around the words you don't recognize.

MASTER WORDS

chute	descent	flail	hurtle	scramble
clench	desperate	glimpse	reserve	yowl

Read the selection on the preceding page again, this time paying special attention to the ten Master Words. In the (a) spaces provided below, write down what you think is the meaning of the word. After you have attempted a definition for each word, look up the word in a dictionary. In the (b) spaces, copy the appropriate dictionary definition.

1. **chute** (n.)

   a. ____

   b. _____ an umbrella-shaped device used to slow free fall from an airplane or to slow speeding vehicles (informal for ''parachute'')

2. **clench** (v.)

   a. ____

   b. _____ to close tightly; also, to grasp firmly

3. **descent** (n.)

   a. ____

   b. _____ downward motion

4. **desperate** (adj.)

   a. ____

   b. _____ driven to or produced by hopelessness; reckless, rash, or frantic because of despair

5. **flail** (v.)

   a. ____

   b. _____ to throw one's arms or legs about wildly

6. **glimpse** (n.)

   a. ____

   b. _____ a hurried view

7. **hurtle** (v.)

   a. ____

   b. _____ to move with great speed

8. **reserve** (adj.)

   a. ____

   b. _____ extra, as something kept back or saved

9. **scramble** (v.)

   a. ____

   b. _____ to hurriedly and often clumsily struggle to get something

10. **yowl** (v.)

   a. ____

   b. _____ to give a long, loud, mournful cry

Use the following list of synonyms and antonyms to fill in the blanks. Some words have no antonyms. In such cases, the antonym blanks have been marked with an X.

clutch	dawdle	fling	howl	rise	spent
confident	extra	frantic	parachute	rush	stare
creep	fall	glance	release	scurry	whisper

	Synonyms	**Antonyms**
1. **clench**	(clutch)	(release)
2. **glimpse**	(glance)	(stare)
3. **yowl**	(howl)	(whisper)
4. **desperate**	(frantic)	(confident)
5. **hurtle**	(rush) (scurry)	(creep) (dawdle)
6. **scramble**	(scurry) (rush)	(dawdle) (creep)
7. **reserve**	(extra)	(spent)
8. **flail**	(fling)	X
9. **chute**	(parachute)	X
10. **descent**	(fall)	(rise)

Decide whether the first pair in the items below are synonyms or antonyms. Then choose the Master Word that shows a similar relation to the word(s) preceding the blank.

1. pedestal	:crown	::loosen	: (clench)
2. cloak	:coat	::parachute	: (chute)
3. impractical	:efficient	::gaze	: (glimpse)
4. severe	:tender	::climb	: (descent)
5. mutter	:mumble	::hurry	: (scramble)
6. sapphire	:blue gemstone	::bellow	: (yowl)
7. gilded	:gold-covered	::tumble	: (flail) (hurtle)
8. sensible	:romantic	::calm	: (desperate)
9. reputation	:importance	::spare	: (reserve)
10. councilor	:board member	::tumble	: (hurtle) (flail)

LESSON EIGHTEEN

The Master Words in this lesson are repeated below. From the Master Words, choose the appropriate word for the blank in each of the following sentences. Write the word in the numbered space provided at the right.

chute	descent	flail	hurtle	scramble
clench	desperate	glimpse	reserve	yowl

1. The ...?... man threw all his money on the table to make one last, wild bet.

1. _____ (desperate)

2. Even if we do drink this entire carton of milk, we have a ...?... carton in the cooler.

2. _____ (reserve)

3. She caught a ...?... of the thief but couldn't describe him.

3. _____ (glimpse)

4. After the quarterback fumbled, players from both teams ...?...(d, ed) to recover the loose football.

4. _____ (scramble)

5. ...?...(s) were used to drop food and medical supplies from planes to the victims of the hurricane.

5. _____ (chute)

6. Don's form was so good as he made his ...?... from the diving board that the judges awarded him the full ten points.

6. _____ (descent)

7. The distant ...?... of a coyote broke the silence of the frosty, moonlit night.

7. _____ (yowl)

8. The toddler ...?...(d, ed) the rattle tightly in his fist and shook it.

8. _____ (clench)

9. The clown walking the tightrope ...?...(d, ed) her arms wildly and pretended to lose her balance.

9. _____ (flail)

10. Outdistancing the other racers by 200 yards, the driver of the Porsche ...?...(d, ed) toward the finish line.

10. _____ (hurtle)

Write the Master Word that is associated with each word group below. Then list three things that might be associated with the review word that follows.

1. starving people, last resort, emergency   _____ (desperate)

2. space capsule, aerial acrobat, paratrooper   _____ (chute)

3. off-balance, flapping, drowning   _____ (flail)

4. nest egg, extra keys, spare tire   _____ (reserve)

5. javelin, meteor, shooting star   _____ (hurtle)

6. alarm clock, race, fire drill   _____ (scramble)

7. plane landing, waterfall, sky diver   _____ (descent)

8. cat, someone in pain, coyote   _____ (yowl)

9. peep, brief look, glance   _____ (glimpse)

10. teeth, fist, steering wheel   _____ (clench)

Review word: cloak (Lesson 17)

(Little Red Riding Hood) _____   (Superman) _____   (Dracula) _____

(Note: Answers may vary.)

Read the following selection to get the general meaning. Read it a second time, paying special attention to the words in dark type. Notice how they are used in sentences. These are Master Words. These are the words you will be working with in this lesson.

From **Arabian Nights**

"I **rebelled** against the King of the Genii," [the **genie** began]. "To punish me, he shut me up in this vase of copper and put on its leaden cover his seal, which is **enchantment** enough to prevent my coming out. Then he had the vase thrown into the sea. During the first period of my **captivity** I **vowed** that if anyone should free me before a hundred years passed, I would make him rich even after his death. But that century passed and no one freed me. In the second century I vowed I would give all the treasures in the world to my **deliverer**; but he never came.

"In the third, I promised to make him a king, to be always near him and to grant him three wishes every day; but that century passed away as the other two had and I remained in the same **plight**. At last I grew angry at being a captive for so long and vowed that if anyone would release me I would kill him and would only allow him to choose in what manner he should die. As you have freed me today, choose in what way you will die."

The fisherman was very unhappy. "What an unlucky man I am to have freed you! I **implore** you to spare my life."

"I have told you," said the genie, "that is impossible. Choose quickly; you are wasting time."

The fisherman began to **devise** a plot. "Since I must die," he said, "before I choose the manner of my death, I **conjure** you on your honor to tell me if you really were in that vase?"

"Yes, I was," answered the genie.

"I really cannot believe it," said the fisherman. "That vase could not contain one of your feet even, and how could it hold your whole body? I cannot believe it unless I see you go into the vase."

Then the genie began to change himself into smoke which, as before, spread over the sea and the shore and then, collecting itself together, began to go back into the vase slowly and evenly till there was nothing left outside. Then a voice came from the vase, which said to the fisherman, "Well, unbelieving fisherman, here I am in the vase. Do you believe me now?"

The fisherman, instead of answering, took the lid of lead and shut it down quickly on the vase.

EXERCISE 1

SELF-TEST: After reading the above selection, do the following. Look at the Master Words below. Underline the words that you think you know. Circle the words that you are less sure about. Draw a square around the words you don't recognize.

MASTER WORDS

captivity	**genie**
conjure	**implore**
deliverer	**plight**
devise	**rebel**
enchantment	**vow**

Read the selection on the preceding page again, this time paying special attention to the ten Master Words. In the (a) spaces provided below, write down what you think is the meaning of the word. After you have attempted a definition for each word, look up the word in a dictionary. In the (b) spaces, copy the appropriate dictionary definition.

1. **captivity** (n.)

   a. ___________________________________

   b. ___ imprisonment; bondage; confinement ___

2. **conjure** (v.)

   a. ___________________________________

   b. ___ to solemnly request, beg, or appeal to ___

3. **deliverer** (n.)

   a. ___________________________________

   b. ___ one who rescues or releases another from an unpleasant or dangerous situation; a liberator ___

4. **devise** (v.)

   a. ___________________________________

   b. ___ to think out; to plan; to scheme ___

5. **enchantment** (n.)

   a. ___________________________________

   b. ___ a magical spell or charm ___

6. **genie** (n.)

   a. ___________________________________

   b. ___ a spirit of Moslem mythology that works magic (also spelled jinni) ___

7. **implore** (v.)

   a. ___________________________________

   b. ___ to call upon, as for help; to beseech; to entreat; to beg ___

8. **plight** (n.)

   a. ___________________________________

   b. ___ a state or situation, usually bad ___

9. **rebel** (v.)

   a. ___________________________________

   b. ___ to resist or oppose authority ___

10. **vow** (v.)

   a. ___________________________________

   b. ___ to promise solemnly ___

Use the following list of synonyms and antonyms to fill in the blanks. Some words have no antonyms. In such cases, the antonym blanks have been marked with an X.

assist	captor	imprisonment	plan	refuse	solution
beg	freedom	improvise	predicament	rescuer	spirit
beseech	grant	magic	promise	revolt	submit

	Synonyms	**Antonyms**
1. **rebel**	(revolt)	(submit)
2. **genie**	(spirit)	X
3. **enchantment**	(magic)	X
4. **captivity**	(imprisonment)	(freedom)
5. **vow**	(promise)	(refuse)
6. **deliverer**	(rescuer)	(captor)
7. **plight**	(predicament)	(solution)
8. **implore**	(beseech) (beg)	(grant) (assist)
9. **devise**	(plan)	(improvise)
10. **conjure**	(beg) (beseech)	(assist) (grant)

Decide whether the first pair in the items below are synonyms or antonyms. Then choose the Master Word that shows a similar relation to the word(s) preceding the blank.

1. chute	:parachute	::develop	: (devise)
2. clench	:relax	::jailer	: (deliverer)
3. glimpse	:gawk	::obey	: (rebel)
4. scramble	:scamper	::pledge	: (vow)
5. yowl	:yelp	::demon	: (genie)
6. descent	:ascent	::liberty	: (captivity)
7. desperate	:reckless	::request	: (implore)
8. hurtle	:crawl	::give	: (conjure) (implore)
9. reserve	:unused	::sorcery	: (enchantment)
10. flail	:fling	::difficulty	: (plight)

The Master Words in this lesson are repeated below. From the Master Words, choose the appropriate word for the blank in each of the following sentences. Write the word in the numbered space provided at the right.

captivity	deliverer	enchantment	implore	rebel
conjure	devise	genie	plight	vow

1. Survival in the wilds of nature would be difficult, if not impossible, for animals that were born and raised in ...?... .

   1. ________ (captivity)

2. Carolyn ...?...(d, ed) her teammates to help her search for the contact lens that was somewhere on the locker room floor.

   2. ________ (implore) (conjure)

3. Moses is considered the ...?... of the Israelites, for he is said to have led them out of Egypt after more than 400 years of slavery.

   3. ________ (deliverer)

4. A witness in a court of law must ...?... to tell "the truth, the whole truth, and nothing but the truth."

   4. ________ (vow)

5. Ulysses faced the ...?... of having to sail his ship between the dangerous rock Scylla and the whirlpool Charybdis.

   5. ________ (plight)

6. The fairy king used a magic potion to put the humans under (a, an) ...?... .

   6. ________ (enchantment)

7. When the British Parliament passed the Stamp Act in 1765, American colonists decided to ...?... against such unfair treatment.

   7. ________ (rebel)

8. Coach Wilson tried to ...?... plays that would take the best advantage of the team's tall center and quick forwards.

   8. ________ (devise)

9. The hypnotist told his subject, "I ...?... you, tell us what past lives you have lived."

   9. ________ (conjure) (implore)

10. What would be your commands to (a, an) ...?... who would magically grant you three wishes?

    10. ________ (genie)

To complete the crossword, choose the Master Word associated with each word or phrase below. Begin each answer in the square having the same number as the clue.

1. lifesaver
2. cook up a scheme
3. state of a caged bird
4. a tight spot
5. can mean to request *or* to summon by magic
6. to plead with
7. wizards and witches have this power
8. break the rules
9. "I solemnly swear"
10. may give you three wishes

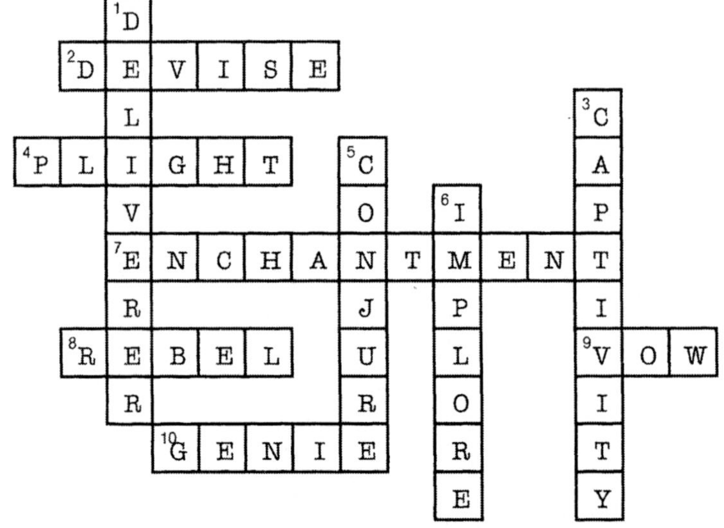

Read the following selection to get the general meaning. Read it a second time, paying special attention to the words in dark type. Notice how they are used in sentences. These are Master Words. These are the words you will be working with in this lesson.

From "**The Revolt of Mother**"
by Mary E. Wilkins Freeman

Sarah Penn's face as she rolled her pies had that **expression** of **meek vigor** which might have **characterized** one of the New Testament saints. She was making mince pies. Her husband, Adoniram Penn, liked them better than any other kind. She baked twice a week. Adoniram often liked a piece of pie between meals. She hurried this morning. It had been later than usual when she began, and she wanted to have a pie baked for dinner. However deep a **resentment** she might be forced to hold against her husband, she would never fail in [devoted] attention to his wants.

Nobility of character **manifests** itself at **loopholes** when it is not provided with large doors. Sarah Penn's showed itself today in flaky dishes of pastry. So she made the pies faithfully, while across the table she could see, when she glanced up from her work, the sight that **rankled** in her patient and **steadfast** soul— the digging of the cellar of the new barn in the place where Adoniram forty years ago had promised her their new house should stand.

The pies were done for dinner. Adoniram and Sammy were home a few minutes after twelve o'clock. The dinner was eaten with serious haste. There was never much conversation at the table in the Penn family. Adoniram asked a blessing, and they ate promptly, then rose up and went about their work.

EXERCISE 1

SELF-TEST: After reading the above selection, do the following. Look at the Master Words below. Underline the words that you think you know. Circle the words that you are less sure about. Draw a square around the words you don't recognize.

MASTER WORDS

characterize	**nobility**
expression	**rankle**
loophole	**resentment**
manifest	**steadfast**
meek	**vigor**

Read the selection on the preceding page again, this time paying special attention to the ten Master Words. In the (a) spaces provided below, write down what you think is the meaning of the word. After you have attempted a definition for each word, look up the word in a dictionary. In the (b) spaces, copy the appropriate dictionary definition.

1. **characterize** (v.)

   a. ____

   b. to mark or distinguish; to indicate a particular quality

2. **expression** (n.)

   a. ____

   b. a look on the face that reveals one's feelings

3. **loophole** (n.)

   a. ____

   b. a small opening that offers a means of defense or escape

4. **manifest** (v.)

   a. ____

   b. to make evident or obvious; to reveal; to show

5. **meek** (adj.)

   a. ____

   b. mild-tempered; patient; gentle

6. **nobility** (n.)

   a. ____

   b. quality of being worthy or high in rank, mind, or character

7. **rankle** (v.)

   a. ____

   b. to keep within the mind irritation or resentment that becomes increasingly painful

8. **resentment** (n.)

   a. ____

   b. anger or displeasure due to an injury or insult

9. **steadfast** (adj.)

   a. ____

   b. faithful; loyal; true; fixed or unchanging

10. **vigor** (n.)

   a. ____

   b. mental or physical strength or energy

Use the following list of synonyms and antonyms to fill in the blanks. Some words have no antonyms. In such cases, the antonym blanks have been marked with an X.

anger	deadpan	gratitude	look	obstacle	reveal
baseness	disloyal	greatness	mark	opening	soothe
bother	energy	humble	misrepresent	proud	weakness
conceal	faithful				

	Synonyms	**Antonyms**
1. **expression**	(look)	(deadpan)
2. **meek**	(humble)	(proud)
3. **vigor**	(energy)	(weakness)
4. **characterize**	(mark)	(misrepresent)
5. **resentment**	(anger)	(gratitude)
6. **nobility**	(greatness)	(baseness)
7. **manifest**	(reveal)	(conceal)
8. **loophole**	(opening)	(obstacle)
9. **rankle**	(bother)	(soothe)
10. **steadfast**	(faithful)	(disloyal)

Decide whether the first pair in the items below are synonyms or antonyms. Then choose the Master Word that shows a similar relation to the word(s) preceding the blank.

1. devise	:create	::appearance	: (expression)
2. vow	:swear	::irritate	: (rankle)
3. deliverer	:slave driver	::unfaithful	: (steadfast)
4. rebel	:accept	::hide	: (manifest)
5. genie	:spirit	::dignity	: (nobility)
6. captivity	:independence	::overbearing	: (meek)
7. conjure	:ask	::bitterness	: (resentment)
8. implore	:bestow	::barrier	: (loophole)
9. enchantment	:wizardry	::distinguish	: (characterize)
10. plight	:trouble	::strength	: (vigor)

EXERCISE 5 ■■■■■■■■■

The Master Words in this lesson are repeated below. From the Master Words, choose the appropriate word for the blank in each of the following sentences. Write the word in the numbered space provided at the right.

| characterize | loophole | meek | rankle | steadfast |
| expression | manifest | nobility | resentment | vigor |

1. Hector felt refreshed and full of ...?... after a good night's rest.

1. _____ (vigor)

2. Janice felt ...?... growing because, although the best qualified, she was not chosen for the lead in the school play.

2. _____ (resentment)

3. Mother didn't have to ask if we had won the game; she could tell from our gloomy ...?...(s) that we had lost.

3. _____ (expression)

4. A willingness to make fools of themselves is what ...?...(s) most of the winners on that game show.

4. _____ (characterize)

5. Joe meant no harm by his careless comment, but the more I thought about it, the more it ...?...(d, ed) me.

5. _____ (rankle)

6. Although a man of humble birth, Abraham Lincoln was known for his ...?... of character.

6. _____ (nobility)

7. Even when the team made a poor showing, the Pep Club was ...?... in its support.

7. _____ (steadfast)

8. Margo had kept a cheerful attitude throughout her brother's illness, but suddenly her concern ...?...(d, ed) itself in tears.

8. _____ (manifest)

9. The lawyer could not find one ...?... in the law to save her client from going to prison.

9. _____ (loophole)

10. Walter Mitty was (a, an) ...?... man who was daring only in his romantic dreams.

10. _____ (meek)

EXERCISE 6 ■■■■■■■■■

Order the words in each item from *least* to *most*. Use the abbreviations *L* for "least" and *M* for "most." Leave the line before the word of the middle degree blank. The first word provides a clue about how to arrange the words. See the example.

sanitary: __M__ disinfected _____ scrubbed __L__ washed
(*Washed* indicates the least sanitary; *disinfected* indicates the most sanitary.)

1. detailed: _____ characterize __(L)__ sketch __(M)__ dissect

2. irritation: __(M)__ anger _____ resentment __(L)__ displeasure

3. energy: _____ strength __(M)__ vigor __(L)__ fatigue

4. worthiness: _____ goodness __(L)__ phoniness __(M)__ nobility

5. constant: __(M)__ steadfast __(L)__ unfaithful _____ wavering

6. annoyed: __(M)__ enrage _____ rankle __(L)__ ruffle

7. emotional: _____ expression __(M)__ outburst __(L)__ poker face

8. chance for freedom: __(M)__ exit __(L)__ loophole _____ escape hatch

9. hidden: __(L)__ manifest _____ veiled __(M)__ invisible

10. bold: __(L)__ meek __(M)__ aggressive _____ confident

(Note: In some cases, answers may vary.)

Read the following selection to get the general meaning. Read it a second time, paying special attention to the words in dark type. Notice how they are used in sentences. These are Master Words. These are the words you will be working with in this lesson.

Adapted from **The Land of Oz**
by L. Frank Baum

"It is but honest that I should **acknowledge** at the beginning of my **recital** that I was born an ordinary Woggle-Bug," began the creature, in a **frank** and friendly tone. "Knowing no better, I used my arms as well as my legs for walking, and crawled under the edges of stones or hid among the roots of grasses with no thought beyond finding a few insects smaller than myself to feed upon.

"The chill nights **rendered** me stiff and motionless, for I wore no clothing, but each morning the warm rays of the sun gave me new life and **restored** me to activity. A horrible **existence** is this, but you must remember it is the regularly **ordained** existence of Woggle-Bugs, as well as of many other tiny creatures that **inhabit** the earth.

"But **Destiny** had **singled** me out, humble though I was, for a grander fate! One day I crawled near to a country school house, and my curiosity being excited by the hum of the students within, I made bold to enter and creep along a crack between two boards until I reached the far end, where, in front of a warm fireplace, sat the master at his desk.

"No one noticed so small a creature as a Woggle-Bug, and when I found that the fireplace was even warmer and more comfortable than the sunshine, I decided to establish my future home beside it. So I found a charming nest between two bricks and hid myself therein for many, many months.

"Professor Nowitall is, doubtless, the most famous scholar in the land of Oz, and after a few days I began to listen to the lectures he gave his pupils. Not one of the pupils paid more attention than the humble, unnoticed Woggle-Bug, and I acquired in this way an amount of knowledge that is simply remarkable. That is why I place 'T.E.'—Thoroughly Educated—upon my cards."

EXERCISE 1

SELF-TEST: After reading the above selection, do the following. Look at the Master Words below. Underline the words that you think you know. Circle the words that you are less sure about. Draw a square around the words you don't recognize.

MASTER WORDS

acknowledge	ordain
destiny	recital
existence	render
frank	restore
inhabit	single

Read the selection on the preceding page again, this time paying special attention to the ten Master Words. In the (a) spaces provided below, write down what you think is the meaning of the word. After you have attempted a definition for each word, look up the word in a dictionary. In the (b) spaces, copy the appropriate dictionary definition.

1. **acknowledge** (v.)

   a. ____

   b. _____ to recognize and accept as a fact; to admit _____

2. **destiny** (n.)

   a. ____

   b. _____ the power or force said to determine the course of events _____

3. **existence** (n.)

   a. ____

   b. _____ the manner of living; also, the state of being alive _____

4. **frank** (adj.)

   a. ____

   b. _____ truthful and open in speech; outspoken; candid; sincere _____

5. **inhabit** (v.)

   a. ____

   b. _____ to live in; to make one's home in _____

6. **ordain** (v.)

   a. ____

   b. _____ to establish by law, decree, or destiny _____

7. **recital** (n.)

   a. ____

   b. _____ the act of telling a story, usually to an audience _____

8. **render** (v.)

   a. ____

   b. _____ to cause to be or become; to make _____

9. **restore** (v.)

   a. ____

   b. _____ to return to an earlier condition; to renew _____

10. **single** (v.)

   a. ____

   b. _____ (usually used with "out") to select from among a group; to set apart _____

Use the following list of synonyms and antonyms to fill in the blanks. Some words have no antonyms. In such cases, the antonym blanks have been marked with an X.

account	death	deny	life	overlook	secretive
admit	decay	fate	make	pick	vacate
candid	decree	free choice	occupy	renew	

	Synonyms	**Antonyms**
1. **acknowledge**	(admit)	(deny)
2. **recital**	(account)	X
3. **frank**	(candid)	(secretive)
4. **render**	(make)	X
5. **restore**	(renew)	(decay)
6. **existence**	(life)	(death)
7. **ordain**	(decree)	X
8. **inhabit**	(occupy)	(vacate)
9. **destiny**	(fate)	(free choice)
10. **single**	(pick)	(overlook)

Decide whether the first pair in the items below are synonyms or antonyms. Then choose the Master Word that shows a similar relation to the word(s) preceding the blank.

1. steadfast	:unreliable	::dishonest	: (frank)
2. expression	:manner	::cause	: (render)
3. manifest	:cover	::ruin	: (restore)
4. rankle	:annoy	::establish	: (ordain)
5. meek	:conceited	::abandon	: (inhabit)
6. resentment	:appreciation	::extinction	: (existence)
7. nobility	:decency	::choose	: (single)
8. loophole	:blockage	::ignore	: (acknowledge)
9. characterize	:describe	::telling	: (recital)
10. vigor	:power	::chance	: (destiny)

LESSON TWENTY-ONE

The Master Words in this lesson are repeated below. From the Master Words, choose the appropriate word for the blank in each of the following sentences. Write the word in the numbered space provided at the right.

acknowledge	existence	inhabit	recital	restore
destiny	frank	ordain	render	single

1. Historic buildings in Williamsburg, Virginia, have been ...?...(d, ed) to appear as they did in colonial days.

1. _______ (restore)

2. Although they had won the game, the team members had to ...?... that they had not played as well as usual.

2. _______ (acknowledge)

3. Grandpa's ...?... of his part in the rescue operation grew more dramatic with each retelling.

3. _______ (recital)

4. Scouts who attended our school talent show ...?...(d, ed) out Marcia as "most promising."

4. _______ (single)

5. The last person who ...?...(d, ed) this ghost town left over seventy years ago.

5. _______ (inhabit)

6. Some people believe what their horoscopes ...?... for their lives.

6. _______ (ordain)

7. Miss Winters welcomed the students' ...?..., honest comments on how to improve her course in American literature.

7. _______ (frank)

8. Elise was ...?...(d, ed) speechless when Andrew suddenly confessed that he loved her.

8. _______ (render)

9. Some people in America have a miserable ...?... because they lack proper food, clothing, and shelter.

9. _______ (existence)

10. Do you think our lives are shaped by ...?..., or do we determine our own fates?

10. _______ (destiny)

To complete the word spiral, choose the Master Word associated with each phrase below. Start with 1 and fill in each answer clockwise. Be careful! Each new word may overlap the previous word by one or more letters.

1. open and honest

2. what will be, will be

3. to cause or bring about

4. put into good repair

5. detailed narration of facts

6. own up to

7. call attention to

8. life and breath

9. make a rule or law

10. live in a house, for example

1. F	R	A	N	K	2. D	E	S	T
6. A	C	K	N	O	W	L	E	I
L	N	C	E	9. O	R	D	D	N
A	E					A	G	Y
T	T	T				10. I	E	3. R
I	S	I	B	A	H	N	7. S	E
C	I	X	8. E	L	G	N	I	N
E	5. R	O	T	S	E	4. R	E	D

LESSON 22

Read the following selection to get the general meaning. Read it a second time, paying special attention to the words in dark type. Notice how they are used in sentences. These are Master Words. These are the words you will be working with in this lesson.

From **Five Little Peppers and How They Grew** by Margaret Sidney

"We never had a Christmas," said little Davie reflectively. "What are they like, Jasper?"

Jasper sat quite still, and didn't reply to this question for a moment or two.

To be among children who didn't like Thanksgiving, and who never had seen a Christmas and didn't know what it was like, was a **revelation** to him.

"They hang up stockings," said Polly softly.

How many many times she had begged her mother to try it for the younger ones; but there was never anything to put in them, and the winters were cold and hard, and only the **strictest economy** carried them through.

"Oh!" said little Phronsie in horror, "are their feet in 'em, Polly?"

"No, dear," said Polly, while Jasper, instead of laughing, only stared. Something requiring a deal of thought was passing through the boy's mind just then. "They *shall* have a Christmas!" he muttered. "I know father'll let me." But he kept his thoughts to himself; and becoming his own gay, kindly self, he explained, and told to Phronsie and the others so many stories of past Christmases he had enjoyed that the interest over the baking soon **dwindled** away, until a horrible smell of something burning brought them all to their senses.

"Oh! the house is a-burning!" cried Polly. "Oh, get a pail of water!"

" 'Tisn't either," said Jasper, snuffing wisely. "Oh! I know—I forgot all about it—I do beg your pardon." And running to the stove, he knelt down and drew out of the oven a black, odorous mass, which with a **crestfallen** air he brought to Polly.

"I'm no end sorry I made such a mess of it," he said, "I meant it for you."

" 'Tisn't any matter," said Polly kindly.

"And now do you go on," cried Joel and David, both in the same breath, "all about the Tree, you know."

"Yes, yes," said the others, "if you're not tired, Jasper."

"Oh, no," cried their **accommodating** friend, "I love to tell about it. Only wait—let's help Polly clear up first."

So after all **traces** of the **frolic** had been **tidied** up and made nice for the mother's return, they took seats in a circle, and Jasper **regaled** them with [stories and memories] till they felt as if fairyland were nothing to it!

EXERCISE 1

SELF-TEST: After reading the above selection, do the following. Look at the Master Words below. Underline the words that you think you know. Circle the words that you are less sure about. Draw a square around the words you don't recognize.

<table>
<tr><td colspan="3">MASTER WORDS</td></tr>
<tr><td>accommodating</td><td>frolic</td><td>strict</td></tr>
<tr><td>crestfallen</td><td>regale</td><td>tidy</td></tr>
<tr><td>dwindle</td><td>revelation</td><td>trace</td></tr>
<tr><td>economy</td><td></td><td></td></tr>
</table>

     LESSON TWENTY-TWO

Read the selection on the preceding page again, this time paying special attention to the ten Master Words. In the (a) spaces provided below, write down what you think is the meaning of the word. After you have attempted a definition for each word, look up the word in a dictionary. In the (b) spaces, copy the appropriate dictionary definition.

1. **accommodating** (adj.)

   a. ______________________________

   b. ______ eager to please; agreeable; willing to help

2. **crestfallen** (adj.)

   a. ______________________________

   b. ______ dejected; depressed; downcast

3. **dwindle** (v.)

   a. ______________________________

   b. ______ to become less; to fade or waste away

4. **economy** (n.)

   a. ______________________________

   b. ______ careful management of money, materials, or resources so as to avoid waste

5. **frolic** (n.)

   a. ______________________________

   b. ______ merrymaking; fun; carefree time

6. **regale** (v.)

   a. ______________________________

   b. ______ to delight or entertain with something amusing, interesting, or pleasing

7. **revelation** (n.)

   a. ______________________________

   b. ______ something that is disclosed to one who previously had no knowledge of it

8. **strict** (adj.)

   a. ______________________________

   b. ______ governed by closely enforced rules; kept within narrow limits

9. **tidy** (v.)

   a. ______________________________

   b. ______ to make neat or orderly

10. **trace** (n.)

    a. ______________________________

    b. ______ a sign or a mark, often of something no longer present

Use the following list of synonyms and antonyms to fill in the blanks. Some words have no antonyms. In such cases, the antonym blanks have been marked with an X.

bore	disagreeable	evidence	lenient	neaten	secret
cheerful	disclosure	funeral	merrymaking	obliging	thrift
cover-up	downcast	increase	mess	rigid	wastefulness
decrease	entertain				

	Synonyms	**Antonyms**
1. **revelation**	(disclosure)	(secret)
2. **strict**	(rigid)	(lenient)
3. **economy**	(thrift)	(wastefulness)
4. **dwindle**	(decrease)	(increase)
5. **crestfallen**	(downcast)	(cheerful)
6. **accommodating**	(obliging)	(disagreeable)
7. **trace**	(evidence)	(cover-up)
8. **frolic**	(merrymaking)	(funeral)
9. **tidy**	(neaten)	(mess)
10. **regale**	(entertain)	(bore)

Decide whether the first pair in the items below are synonyms or antonyms. Then choose the Master Word that shows a similar relation to the word(s) preceding the blank.

1. render	:bring about	::discovery	:	(revelation)
2. frank	:insincere	::work	:	(frolic)
3. ordain	:declare	::disappointed	:	(crestfallen)
4. restore	:destroy	::unfriendly	:	(accommodating)
5. single	:select	::amuse	:	(regale)
6. inhabit	:desert	::overspending	:	(economy)
7. existence	:death	::clutter	:	(tidy)
8. recital	:explanation	::harsh	:	(strict)
9. acknowledge	:recognize	::fade	:	(dwindle)
10. destiny	:fortune	::sign	:	(trace)

LESSON TWENTY-TWO

The Master Words in this lesson are repeated below. From the Master Words, choose the appropriate word for the blank in each of the following sentences. Write the word in the numbered space provided at the right.

accommodating	dwindle	frolic	revelation	tidy
crestfallen	economy	regale	strict	trace

1. Fritz managed to save enough to take a trip to Ireland by practicing careful ...?... .

1. _____ (economy)

2. Jenny had allowed the weeks to ...?... so that now she had only four days to complete the six-week project.

2. _____ (dwindle)

3. Investigators could find no ...?... of the flying saucer that was supposed to have landed in the canyon.

3. _____ (trace)

4. Guests at the feast were splendidly ...?...(d, ed) with tropical food and drink, Hawaiian music, and hula dancers.

4. _____ (regale)

5. Dave came home ...?... after being cut from the wrestling team.

5. _____ (crestfallen)

6. The new playground is a perfect place for the children's ...?... .

6. _____ (frolic)

7. The maitre d' was ...?... and readily agreed to switch our order from prime rib to less expensive chuckburgers.

7. _____ (accommodating)

8. Coach Willis had ...?... training rules, and he sometimes dismissed players who broke those rules.

8. _____ (strict)

9. Mother suggested that if Ben would ...?... his room, he might find the jacket he had misplaced.

9. _____ (tidy)

10. The upset victory of Harry Truman as president in 1948 was (a, an) ...?... to pollsters, who had badly misjudged the number of unhappy farmers in the country.

10. _____ (revelation)

Write the Master Word that is associated with each word group below. Then list three things that might be associated with the review word that follows.

1. autumn leaves, melting ice, setting sun

_____ (dwindle)

2. litter, footprint, fossil

_____ (trace)

3. confession, eye opener, inside information

_____ (revelation)

4. maitre d', host, doorkeeper

_____ (accommodating)

5. a dance, fun and games, a romp

_____ (frolic)

6. losing, getting grounded, rejection

_____ (crestfallen)

7. recycling, compact car, savings

_____ (economy)

8. please, delight, warm someone's heart

_____ (regale)

9. spic-and-span, shipshape, well-organized

_____ (tidy)

10. boot camp, crash diet, Olympic training

_____ (strict)

Review word: expression (Lesson 20)

(frown)	(smile)	(grimace)

(Note: Answers may vary.)

Read the following selection to get the general meaning. Read it a second time, paying special attention to the words in dark type. Notice how they are used in sentences. These are Master Words. These are the words you will be working with in this lesson.

From **Around the World in Eighty Days**
by Jules Verne

Phileas Fogg gazed at the **tempestuous** sea, which seemed to be struggling especially to delay him, with his [**customary**] **tranquillity**. He never changed **countenance** for an instant, though a delay of twenty hours, by making him too late for the Yokohama boat, would almost **inevitably** cause the loss of the **wager**. But this man of nerve [showed] neither impatience nor **annoyance**; it seemed as if the storm were a part of his program, and had been **foreseen**. Aouda was amazed to find him as calm as he had been from the first time she saw him.

Fix did not look at the state of things in the same light. The storm greatly pleased him. His satisfaction would have been complete had the "Rangoon" been forced to retreat before the violence of wind and waves. Each delay filled him with hope, for it became more and more [likely] that Fogg would be obliged to remain some days at Hong Kong; and now the heavens themselves became his **allies**, with the gusts and **squalls**. It mattered not that they made him sea-sick—he made no account of this inconvenience . . . .

EXERCISE 1

SELF-TEST: After reading the above selection, do the following. Look at the Master Words below. Underline the words that you think you know. Circle the words that you are less sure about. Draw a square around the words you don't recognize.

MASTER WORDS

ally	**inevitable**
annoyance	**squall**
countenance	**tempestuous**
customary	**tranquillity**
foresee	**wager**

Read the selection on the preceding page again, this time paying special attention to the ten Master Words. In the (a) spaces provided below, write down what you think is the meaning of the word. After you have attempted a definition for each word, look up the word in a dictionary. In the (b) spaces, copy the appropriate dictionary definition.

1. **ally** (n.)

   a. ____

   b. _____ one who gives another aid or cooperation; a supportive friend or associate _____

2. **annoyance** (n.)

   a. ____

   b. _____ irritation or disturbance; nuisance _____

3. **countenance** (n.)

   a. ____

   b. _____ the expression on the face; appearance; also, the face itself _____

4. **customary** (adj.)

   a. ____

   b. _____ according to the accepted way of doing things; usual; habitual _____

5. **foresee** (v.)

   a. ____

   b. _____ to know or see beforehand; to have a vision of a future event _____

6. **inevitable** (adj.)

   a. ____

   b. _____ impossible to avoid or escape; certain to happen _____

7. **squall** (n.)

   a. ____

   b. _____ a gust of wind, often accompanied by rain, snow, or sleet _____

8. **tempestuous** (adj.)

   a. ____

   b. _____ stormy; violent; blustery _____

9. **tranquillity** (n.)

   a. ____

   b. _____ calmness; peacefulness; quietness _____

10. **wager** (n.)

   a. ____

   b. _____ a bet _____

Use the following list of synonyms and antonyms to fill in the blanks. Some words have no antonyms. In such cases, the antonym blanks have been marked with an X.

avoidable	calm	enemy	gust	predict	stillness
bet	certain	excitement	irritation	rare	supporter
blustery	comfort	expression	peaceful	review	usual

	Synonyms	**Antonyms**
1. **tempestuous**	(blustery)	(peaceful)
2. **customary**	(usual)	(rare)
3. **tranquillity**	(stillness) (calm)	(excitement)
4. **countenance**	(expression)	X
5. **inevitable**	(certain)	(avoidable)
6. **wager**	(bet)	X
7. **annoyance**	(irritation)	(comfort)
8. **foresee**	(predict)	(review)
9. **ally**	(supporter)	(enemy)
10. **squall**	(gust)	(calm) (stillness)

Decide whether the first pair in the items below are synonyms or antonyms. Then choose the Master Word that shows a similar relation to the word(s) preceding the blank.

1. frolic	:toil	::uproar	:	(tranquillity)
2. revelation	:news	::face	:	(countenance)
3. crestfallen	:discouraged	::gamble	:	(wager)
4. accommodating	:impolite	::escapable	:	(inevitable)
5. regale	:fascinate	::stormy	:	(tempestuous)
6. economy	:extravagance	::challenger	:	(ally)
7. tidy	:dirty	::uncommon	:	(customary)
8. strict	:stern	::windstorm	:	(squall)
9. dwindle	:expand	::pleasure	:	(annoyance)
10. trace	:clue	::forecast	:	(foresee)

The Master Words in this lesson are repeated below. From the Master Words, choose the appropriate word for the blank in each of the following sentences. Write the word in the numbered space provided at the right.

| ally | countenance | foresee | squall | tranquillity |
| annoyance | customary | inevitable | tempestuous | wager |

1. A turkey dinner with all the trimmings is ...?... for many American families on Thanksgiving Day.

2. In spite of many differences, the United States was (a, an) ...?... of the Soviet Union in both world wars.

3. The sudden ...?... sent us scurrying below deck toward the dryness and security of the ship's cabin.

4. Phileas Fogg made a bold ...?... that he could travel around the world in eighty days.

5. Christopher Columbus did not ...?... that his voyage "around the world" would result in the discovery of a new continent.

6. The feedback from the microphone was (a, an) ...?... to both the speaker and her audience.

7. The eye of a hurricane is a low pressure area characterized by ...?... and, often, clear skies.

8. One look at Tom's ...?... revealed that he, too, had heard the mysterious singing in the creaky old house.

9. Icy streets at rush hour made traffic jams ...?... .

10. The years surrounding the Civil War were a bloody, ...?... period in the history of the United States.

1. _______ (customary)
2. _______ (ally)
3. _______ (squall)
4. _______ (wager)
5. _______ (foresee)
6. _______ (annoyance)
7. _______ (tranquillity)
8. _______ (countenance)
9. _______ (inevitable)
10. _______ (tempestuous)

EXERCISE 6 ▃▃▃▃▃▃▃▃▃▃▃▃▃▃▃▃▃▃▃▃▃▃▃▃▃▃▃▃

Use at least five Master Words from this lesson to write a scene about one of the following topics. Or create a topic of your own. Write your choice on the blank. Circle the Master Words as you use them.

Possible Topics: Feuding Friends, Shopping Mall Nightmare

____

____

____

____

____

____

____

(Note: Answers will vary.)

PART I: From the list below, choose the appropriate word for each sentence that follows. Use each word only once. There will be two words left over.

abandon	descent	engaged	protrude	submerge
characterize	desperate	inhabit	reputation	substantial
customary	dwindle	merciless	serviceable	

1. Penguins are ____________ (characterize) ____________ (d, ed) by short legs, webbed feet, wings which have been reduced to flippers, and a "tuxedo-like" pattern of coloring.

2. (A, An) ____________ (substantial) ____________ breakfast might include juice, eggs, sausage, toast, and milk.

3. Snow and ice forced many travelers to ____________ (abandon) ____________ their cars and seek shelter.

4. If you try to park that huge camper on this narrow street, it will ____________ (protrude) ____________ into the traffic lanes.

5. When a line is busy, the operator says, "That number is ____________ (engaged) ____________."

6. Members of some religious groups believe that true baptism takes place only if the person is ____________ (submerge) ____________ (d, ed) in water.

7. About twenty minutes after takeoff from Kansas City, the pilot announced that we would begin our ____________ (descent) ____________ to land in St. Louis.

8. Though Jack claimed he'd do anything to earn some money, he refused a job as a prison guard, saying he wasn't that ____________ (desperate) ____________.

9. The importance of Wells, Fargo, and Company as a means of cross-country travel ____________ (dwindle) ____________ (d, ed) after the Central-Union Pacific Railroad was completed in 1869.

10. Winston's ____________ (reputation) ____________ suffered when he was falsely accused of a crime, but not his character.

11. The ____________ (merciless) ____________ landlord told the family to leave the apartment though they had nowhere to go but the streets.

12. For adults, the ____________ (customary) ____________ welcome to a newcomer is a handshake.

PART II: Decide whether the first pair in the items below are synonyms or antonyms. Then choose a Master Word from Lessons 13–23 that shows a similar relation to the word(s) preceding the blank. Do not repeat a Master Word that appears in the first column.

1. indefinite :measurable ::foe : ____________ (ally)

2. impractical :senseless ::saving : ____________ (economy)

3. tempestuous :calm ::surrender : ____________ (resistance)

4. bogged :tangled ::confinement : ____________ (captivity)

5. rebel :disobey ::illustrate : ____________ (depict)

(Note: Other answers may be possible.)

  LESSON TWENTY-FOUR

PART III: From the list below, choose the appropriate word for each sentence that follows. Use each word only once. There will be two words left over.

acknowledge	exhaustion	inevitable	rebel	scramble
crestfallen	foresee	instinct	render	severe
devise	frank	preserve	resentment	

1. Following passage of the Homestead Act in 1862, thousands of people __________ (scramble) __________ (d, ed) westward to settle the new frontier.

2. When Tim learned that the student who sold the most magazines would win a trip, he began to __________ (devise) __________ ways of attracting new customers.

3. For the president to __________ (acknowledge) __________ that he had made a mistake was difficult; however, it won him the respect and support of Americans.

4. My __________ (resentment) __________ of Claudia began to fade when I saw she had not meant to hurt my feelings but just give me some helpful tips.

5. Many disagreements can be solved by (a, an) __________ (frank) __________ discussion in which all parties involved express their views clearly and calmly.

6. Some people wanted to combine the two clubs, but the officers believed that each club should __________ (preserve) __________ its own identity.

7. The automobile __________ (render) __________ (d, ed) horse-drawn vehicles obsolete.

8. The American colonists decided to __________ (rebel) __________ against the laws and taxes placed on them by the British.

9. In addition to health and happiness, the palm reader declared that she could __________ (foresee) __________ wealth and travel for me.

10. Growing old is __________ (inevitable) __________; so are death and taxes.

11. Manda expected her punishment would be __________ (severe) __________ after she dented the car, but her parents were very understanding.

12. Rhonda looks __________ (crestfallen) __________—she expected to win that prize.

PART IV: Decide whether the first pair in the items below are synonyms or antonyms. Then choose a Master Word from Lessons 13–23 that shows a similar relation to the word(s) preceding the blank. Do not repeat a Master Word that appears in the first column.

1. goad   :push   ::make known   : __________ (manifest) __________

2. accommodating :uncooperative ::fairness   : __________ (injustice) __________

3. meek   :obedient   ::dedicated   : __________ (steadfast) __________

4. implore   :ask   ::luck   : __________ (destiny) __________

5. portly   :plump   ::last-mentioned   : __________ (latter) __________

(Note: Other answers may be possible.)

Read the following selection to get the general meaning. Read it a second time, paying special attention to the words in dark type. Notice how they are used in sentences. These are Master Words. These are the words you will be working with in this lesson.

Adapted from **"A Little Cloud"** from **Dubliners** by James Joyce

Little Chandler's thoughts ever since lunchtime had been of his meeting with Gallaher, of Gallaher's invitation and of the great city London where Gallaher lived. He was called Little Chandler because, though he was but slightly under the average **stature**, he gave one the idea of being a little man. His hands were white and small, his frame was **fragile**, his voice was quiet and his manners were **refined**. He took the greatest care of his fair silken hair and moustache and used perfume **discreetly** on his handkerchief. The halfmoons of his nails were [**flawless**] and when he smiled you caught a glimpse of a row of childish white teeth.

As he sat at his desk in the King's Inns he thought what changes those eight years had brought. The friend whom he had known under a **shabby guise** had become a brilliant figure of the London Press. He turned often from his tiresome writing to gaze out of the office window. The glow of a late autumn sunset covered the grass plots and walks. It cast a shower of kindly golden dust on the untidy nurses and **decrepit** old men who **drowsed** on the benches; it **flickered** upon all the moving figures—on the children who ran screaming along the gravel paths and on everyone who passed through the gardens. He watched the scene and thought of life; and (as always happened when he thought of life) he became sad.

EXERCISE 1

SELF-TEST: After reading the above selection, do the following. Look at the Master Words below. Underline the words that you think you know. Circle the words that you are less sure about. Draw a square around the words you don't recognize.

MASTER WORDS

decrepit	**fragile**
discreet	**guise**
drowse	**refined**
flawless	**shabby**
flicker	**stature**

Read the selection on the preceding page again, this time paying special attention to the ten Master Words. In the (a) spaces provided below, write down what you think is the meaning of the word. After you have attempted a definition for each word, look up the word in a dictionary. In the (b) spaces, copy the appropriate dictionary definition.

1. **decrepit** (adj.)

   a. _______________________________________

   b. ____ broken down; worn out or weakened by old age ____

2. **discreet** (adj.)

   a. _______________________________________

   b. ____ showing good judgment in behavior and speech; prudent; cautious ____

3. **drowse** (v.)

   a. _______________________________________

   b. ____ to be half asleep ____

4. **flawless** (adj.)

   a. _______________________________________

   b. ____ without any imperfection; faultless; perfect ____

5. **flicker** (v.)

   a. _______________________________________

   b. ____ to shine with a wavering light; to burn unsteadily ____

6. **fragile** (adj.)

   a. _______________________________________

   b. ____ easily broken; brittle; frail ____

7. **guise** (n.)

   a. _______________________________________

   b. ____ outward appearance, often with the purpose of deceiving or masking ____

8. **refined** (adj.)

   a. _______________________________________

   b. ____ free from crudeness or vulgarity; cultured; polished ____

9. **shabby** (adj.)

   a. _______________________________________

   b. ____ appearing worn out; faded or ragged ____

10. **stature** (n.)

   a. _______________________________________

   b. ____ height of a person or animal ____

Use the following list of synonyms and antonyms to fill in the blanks. Some words have no antonyms. In such cases, the antonym blanks have been marked with an X.

appearance	careful	faulty	height	perfect	robust
awaken	crude	feeble	imprudent	ragged	tough
beam	cultured	frail	neat	reality	waver
breadth	doze				

	Synonyms	**Antonyms**
1. **stature**	(height)	(breadth)
2. **fragile**	(frail) (feeble)	(tough) (robust)
3. **refined**	(cultured)	(crude)
4. **discreet**	(careful)	(imprudent)
5. **shabby**	(ragged)	(neat)
6. **flawless**	(perfect)	(faulty)
7. **guise**	(appearance)	(reality)
8. **decrepit**	(feeble) (frail)	(robust) (tough)
9. **drowse**	(doze)	(awaken)
10. **flicker**	(waver)	(beam)

Decide whether the first pair in the items below are synonyms or antonyms. Then choose the Master Word that shows a similar relation to the word(s) preceding the blank.

1. tranquillity	:unrest	::strong	:	(fragile)
2. countenance	:appearance	::nap	:	(drowse)
3. inevitable	:preventable	::luxurious	:	(shabby)
4. wager	:bet	::image	:	(guise)
5. ally	:opponent	::blaze	:	(flicker)
6. customary	:exceptional	::rough	:	(refined)
7. tempestuous	:violent	::undamaged	:	(flawless)
8. squall	:gale	::size	:	(stature)
9. foresee	:foretell	::weak	:	(decrepit)
10. annoyance	:enjoyment	::careless	:	(discreet)

LESSON TWENTY-FIVE

The Master Words in this lesson are repeated below. From the Master Words, choose the appropriate word for the blank in each of the following sentences. Write the word in the numbered space provided at the right.

decrepit	drowse	flicker	guise	shabby
discreet	flawless	fragile	refined	stature

1. Kenny is determined to play basketball, despite his small ...?... .

    1. ______ (stature)

2. The large, portly woman looked strong, but when she shuffled across the room, we saw that old age had made her ...?... .

    2. ______ (decrepit)

3. The young woman spoke ...?... Italian, reflecting the years of education she had received in Rome.

    3. ______ (flawless)

4. A gentle breeze made the sunlight ...?... through the leaves of the maple tree.

    4. ______ (flicker)

5. Grandmother showed us the ...?... vase that had been hand-painted by her mother many years ago.

    5. ______ (fragile)

6. Because Alice was ...?..., Lenny knew she could be trusted not to repeat the rumor.

    6. ______ (discreet)

7. What could be more relaxing than to read and ...?... in a hammock on a summer afternoon?

    7. ______ (drowse)

8. Mother protested that my clothes looked ...?..., but I assured her they were merely "broken in" and comfortable.

    8. ______ (shabby)

9. The suspect's ...?... of innocence clashed with the evidence that pointed to his guilt.

    9. ______ (guise)

10. George is a man of ...?... taste; he prefers opera to pop music, theater to TV, and steak to hamburger.

    10. ______ (refined)

EXERCISE 6 ■■■■■■■■■■■■■■■■■■■■■■■■■■■■■■■■

To complete the crossword, choose the Master Word associated with each word or phrase below. Begin each answer in the square having the same number as the clue.

1. a perfect diamond is this

2. stamped on a box of new china

3. candle flames do this in a breeze

4. a countenance that may be a mask

5. Paul Bunyan was great in this

6. what abandoned houses soon become

7. old workhorses get this way

8. what pure sugar has been

9. not a tattletale

10. catnap

Read the following selection to get the general meaning. Read it a second time, paying special attention to the words in dark type. Notice how they are used in sentences. These are Master Words. These are the words you will be working with in this lesson.

From "Li Chang's Million"
by Henry Gregor Felsen

I was positive the old **rascal** could speak excellent English. Most of the Chinese **merchants** can, but they do better business with Americans if they pretend they know no English. "It's very badly made," I said, touching the coat.

"Very well made," the Chinese insisted, slipping his hands into the sleeves of his gown. "Most excellent workmanship."

I examined the **garment** carelessly. "Very bad," I said, just for the sake of argument. "See how badly it is sewn. It would be laughed at in America."

I looked up with a **smirk** still on my lips, hoping to **discomfit** the man. But he had moved, and when I looked up, I gazed into a pair of hurt, sad eyes.

Sitting across the room, behind a counter, unnoticed by me until this moment, sat a boy who looked to be no more than six or seven years of age. While the old men had been sitting around drinking tea, he had been working—and had not stopped until I had by word and action **indicated** my low opinion of the way the coat had been sewn.

For a moment I was completely off balance. I let the coat fall from my hand, and felt a sudden rush of shame. For the boy sat on a high stool, and before him on the counter were two squares of fur that he was sewing by hand. I walked over to him. With a small needle, he was making a line of stitches as tiny and even as could be done on any machine. It was his work I had **criticized**.

"Sorry, Junior," I said lightly. "I didn't mean to run down your work."

The boy looked at me in silence. He had the most hurt expression on his face I had ever caused anyone. I looked into his inky-black eyes, and noticed there were shadows under them. I noticed how his smooth little face already showed signs of the tired, **resigned** expression it was growing into. I noticed how his head and shoulders were already bent, and how even when he rested, his back did not straighten. We stared at one another for a long minute—this child whose work I had **sneered** at and I—and then one of the men spoke to him and he bowed his head and his small fingers took up their slow, **painstaking** stitching again.

EXERCISE 1

SELF-TEST: After reading the above selection, do the following. Look at the Master Words below. Underline the words that you think you know. Circle the words that you are less sure about. Draw a square around the words you don't recognize.

MASTER WORDS

criticize	**merchant**	**resigned**
discomfit	**painstaking**	**smirk**
garment	**rascal**	**sneer**
indicate		

Read the selection on the preceding page again, this time paying special attention to the ten Master Words. In the (a) spaces provided below, write down what you think is the meaning of the word. After you have attempted a definition for each word, look up the word in a dictionary. In the (b) spaces, copy the appropriate dictionary definition.

1. **criticize** (v.)

   a. ____

   b. _____ to judge, especially unfavorably; to find fault with

2. **discomfit** (v.)

   a. ____

   b. _____ to throw into a state of confusion or embarrassment

3. **garment** (n.)

   a. ____

   b. _____ any article of clothing

4. **indicate** (v.)

   a. ____

   b. _____ to make known; to show; also, to point out

5. **merchant** (n.)

   a. ____

   b. _____ one who buys and sells goods for profit; a storekeeper or shopkeeper

6. **painstaking** (adj.)

   a. ____

   b. _____ involving great care and concentration

7. **rascal** (n.)

   a. ____

   b. _____ a mischievous or dishonest person

8. **resigned** (adj.)

   a. ____

   b. _____ showing patient acceptance of a bad, tiring, etc., situation; accepting; meek

9. **smirk** (n.)

   a. ____

   b. _____ a self-satisfied or gloating smile

10. **sneer** (v.)

   a. ____

   b. _____ to express scorn or contempt

Use the following list of synonyms and antonyms to fill in the blanks. Some words have no antonyms. In such cases, the antonym blanks have been marked with an X.

accepting	condemn	embarrass	praise	saint	show
careless	customer	grin	rebellious	scoff	soothe
clothing	diligent	hide	respect	scoundrel	storekeeper

	Synonyms	**Antonyms**
1. **rascal**	(scoundrel)	(saint)
2. **merchant**	(storekeeper)	(customer)
3. **garment**	(clothing)	X
4. **smirk**	(grin)	X
5. **discomfit**	(embarrass)	(soothe)
6. **indicate**	(show)	(hide)
7. **criticize**	(condemn)	(praise)
8. **resigned**	(accepting)	(rebellious)
9. **sneer**	(scoff)	(respect)
10. **painstaking**	(diligent)	(careless)

Decide whether the first pair in the items below are synonyms or antonyms. Then choose the Master Word that shows a similar relation to the word(s) preceding the blank.

1. drowse	:snooze	::apparel	: (garment)
2. fragile	:sturdy	::inexact	: (painstaking)
3. guise	:mask	::disturb	: (discomfit)
4. flawless	:ideal	::disapprove	: (criticize)
5. stature	:height	::smile	: (smirk)
6. decrepit	:sickly	::reveal	: (indicate)
7. shabby	:grand	::compliment	: (sneer) (smirk)
8. flicker	:glow	::resistant	: (resigned)
9. refined	:unpolished	::angel	: (rascal)
10. discreet	:hasty	::shopper	: (merchant)

　　　　　　　　　　　　　　　LESSON TWENTY-SIX

The Master Words in this lesson are repeated below. From the Master Words, choose the appropriate word for the blank in each of the following sentences. Write the word in the numbered space provided at the right.

| criticize | garment | merchant | rascal | smirk |
| discomfit | indicate | painstaking | resigned | sneer |

1. Frank was ...?... to the fact that he would never be a great athlete, though he liked playing sports.

1. _____ (resigned)

2. Nothing pleases that movie reviewer; she has ...?...(d, ed) every film she's written about this year.

2. _____ (criticize)

3. The ...?...(s) in the shopping center hoped to attract many customers with a "Moonlight Madness" sale.

3. _____ (merchant)

4. The style and color of the ...?... were not particularly flattering to Patti's slender figure and olive complexion.

4. _____ (garment)

5. The official scoreboard ...?...(d, ed) that the score was still tied at the end of the first overtime.

5. _____ (indicate)

6. Restringing the pearl necklace was indeed (a, an) ...?... task.

6. _____ (painstaking)

7. Roger resented Karyn's attempt to ...?... him, and he told her not to put him on the spot like that again.

7. _____ (discomfit)

8. Amy displayed a satisfied ...?... after she won the wager.

8. _____ (smirk)

9. Rhett Butler was (a, an) ...?... who dared to do what he pleased no matter how he offended other people.

9. _____ (rascal)

10. Some down-to-earth people ...?... at those who believe that space exploration is important.

10. _____ (sneer)

Fill in the chart below with the Master Word that fits each set of clues. Part of speech refers to the word's usage in the lesson. Use a dictionary when necessary.

Number of Syllables	Part of Speech	Other Clues		Master Word
3	verb	confuse or upset	1.	(discomfit)
2	adjective	like one who's given up	2.	(resigned)
1	noun	gloating expression	3.	(smirk)
2	noun	a coat or other type of dress	4.	(garment)
3	adjective	"sparing no pains"	5.	(painstaking)
2	noun	troublemaker	6.	(rascal)
3	verb	nit-pick	7.	(criticize)
1	verb	turn up your nose at	8.	(sneer)
2	noun	store owner	9.	(merchant)
3	verb	turn signals do this	10.	(indicate)

Read the following selection to get the general meaning. Read it a second time, paying special attention to the words in dark type. Notice how they are used in sentences. These are Master Words. These are the words you will be working with in this section.

from **Annie John**
by Jamaica Kincaid

From time to time, my mother would **fix** on a certain place in our house and give it a good cleaning. If I was home when she happened to do this, I was at her side, as usual. When she did this with the trunk, it was a **tremendous** pleasure, for after she had removed all the things from the trunk, and **aired** them out, and changed the **camphor** balls, and then refolded the things and put them back in their places in the trunk, as she held each thing in her hand she would tell me a story about myself. Sometimes I knew the story first hand, for I could remember the **incident** quite well; sometimes what she told me had happened when I was too young to know anything; and sometimes it happened before I was even born. Whichever way, I knew exactly what she would say, for I had heard it so many times before, but I never got tired of it. For **instance**, the flowers on the **chemise**, the first garment I wore after being born, were not put on correctly, and that is because when my mother was **embroidering** them I kicked so much that her hand was **unsteady**. My mother said that usually when I kicked around in her stomach and she told me to stop I would, but on that day I paid no attention at all. When she told me this story, she would smile at me and say, "You see, even then you were hard to **manage**." It pleased me to think that, before she could see my face, my mother spoke to me in the same way she did now.

EXERCISE 1

SELF-TEST: After reading the above selection, do the following. Look at the Master Words below. Underline the words that you think you know. Circle the words that you are less sure about. Draw a square around the words you don't recognize.

MASTER WORDS

aired	**incident**
camphor	**instance**
chemise	**manage**
embroidering	**tremendous**
fix	**unsteady**

Read the selection on the preceding page again, this time paying special attention to the ten Master Words. In the (a) spaces provided below, write down what you think is the meaning of the word. After you have attempted a definition for each word, look up the word in a dictionary. In the (b) spaces, copy the appropriate dictionary definition.

1. **aired** (v.)

    a. ____

    b. ___ freshened by exposing to the air _______________

2. **camphor** (n.)

    a. ____

    b. ___ insect repellent made from the camphor tree _____

3. **chemise** (n.)

    a. ____

    b. ___ undergarment _________________________________

4. **embroidering** (v.)

    a. ____

    b. ___ decorating with needlework ___________________

5. **fix** (v.)

    a. ____

    b. ___ direct one's attention; focus _________________

6. **incident** (n.)

    a. ____

    b. ___ minor occurrence dependent on something else ___

7. **instance** (n.)

    a. ____

    b. ___ example ____________________________________

8. **manage** (v.)

    a. ____

    b. ___ handle or control ____________________________

9. **tremendous** (adj.)

    a. ____

    b. ___ unusually large; huge ________________________

10. **unsteady** (adj.)

    a. ____

    b. ___ not stable; shaky ____________________________

Use the following list of synonyms and antonyms to fill in the blanks. Some of the words have no antonyms. In such cases, the antonym blanks have been marked with an X.

buried	freshened	mishandle	shaky	stitching
example	handle	occurrence	small	undergarment
focus	huge	repellent	stable	

	Synonyms	**Antonyms**
1. **fix**	(focus)	X
2. **tremendous**	(huge)	(small)
3. **aired**	(freshened)	(buried)
4. **camphor**	(repellent)	X
5. **incident**	(occurrence or example)	X
6. **instance**	(example or occurrence)	X
7. **chemise**	(undergarment)	X
8. **embroidering**	(stitching)	X
9. **unsteady**	(shaky)	(stable)
10. **manage**	(handle)	(mishandle)

Decide whether the first pair in the items below are synonyms or antonyms. Then choose the Master Word that shows a similar relation to the word(s) preceding the blank.

1. infinite	:endless	::stitching	:	(embroidering)
2. representatives	:delegates	::event	:	(incident)
3. sacred	:defiled	::insignificant	:	(tremendous)
4. plan	:agenda	::focus	:	(fix)
5. good will	:rancor	::steady	:	(unsteady)
6. watchful	:vigilant	::example	:	(instance)
7. lasting	:durable	::exposed to air	:	(aired)
8. petition	:appeal	::control	:	(manage)
9. paradox	:contradiction	::repellent	:	(camphor)
10. restrict	:prohibit	::underwear	:	(chamise)

The Master Words in this lesson are repeated below. From the Master Words, choose the appropriate word for the blank in each of the following sentences. Write the word in the numbered space provided at the right.

| aired | chemise | fix | instance | tremendous |
| camphor | embroidering | incident | manage | unsteady |

1. They had a ...?... amount of respect for this courageous woman.

1. _____ (tremendous) _____

2. The horse was difficult to ...?... at first, but relaxed as it got to know its rider.

2. _____ (manage) _____

3. The unpleasant ...?... with two strangers left him with a sad memory and a new wariness of unknown people.

3. _____ (incident) _____

4. She hung the curtains on the clothesline and ...?... them out in the fresh spring breeze.

4. _____ (aired) _____

5. If she were to ...?... her gaze on you, you would feel nervous too.

5. _____ (fix) _____

6. Their encounter with the vicious dog was a good ...?... of "beware of the dog."

6. _____ (instance) _____

7. The smell of ...?... burned in his nose; no wonder the insects stayed away!

7. _____ (camphor) _____

8. The lacy ...?... would be the perfect gift for her mother, who never bought pretty things for herself.

8. _____ (chemise) _____

9. His grandmother was busy ...?... a tablecloth to use at the anniversary party.

9. _____ (embroidering) _____

10. Linda felt a little ...?... after her fall, but luckily, she was not badly hurt.

10. _____ (unsteady) _____

Find the Master Words in the puzzle to the right.

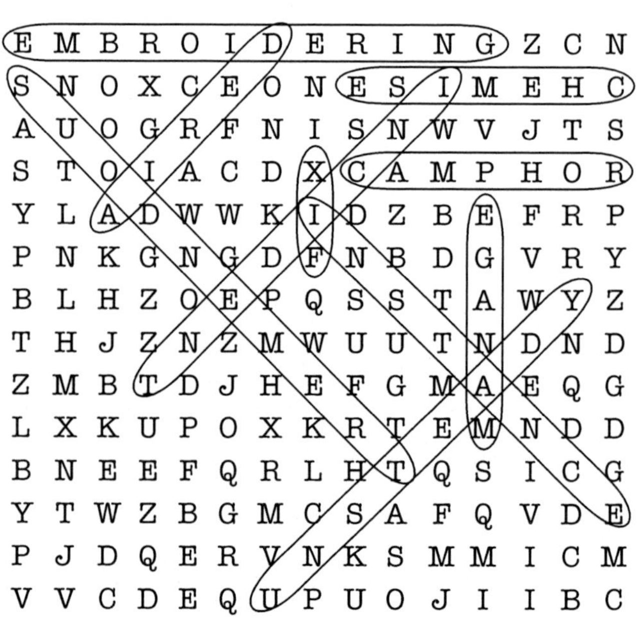

Read the following selection to get the general meaning. Read it a second time, paying special attention to the words in dark type. Notice how they are used in sentences. These are Master Words. These are the words you will be working with in this lesson.

Adapted from **The Nitty Gritty**
by Frank Bonham

When Caesar finally arrived, he got straight to work as though **perspiration** might go out of style before dark. The two of them made a big hole in the wall. Whenever a rat showed its head one of them would **snatch** up the rifle and knock it off. Resting from brickwork, they turned up some hub caps, a couple of dozen wine bottles, and two automobile generators that might have a little value. The sun sank behind the **reservoir**, and the sky darkened to the color of crankcase drainings.

Charlie found a soggy doll. Tired, he sat on the wall and looked at it. It had no hair or lashes, but its eyes were bright blue. It put him in mind of an old woman who had been beautiful and thought she still was.

"Ouch!" someone called, breaking his fantasy. Charlie came blinking back to life to see Caesar standing in the middle of the darkening lot.

"What's the matter?" Charlie called.

"I stubbed my toe on something. It looks like a chunk of bronze or iron."

"Prob'ly a safe full of money," Charlie said. He joined him, and with scraps of metal they dug it up. What Caesar had stumbled on was a long metal box, badly **corroded** but still wearing patches of black paint.

"Strongbox, maybe!" Caesar said.

"No, it's more likely a Mickey Mouse lunchbox with the original sandwich," Charlie suggested.

The box, however, was as solid as stone. They turned it over. "Hey!" Charlie exclaimed. "It's a pay phone!"

The telephone was of a very old type, the cord rotted away and the receiver a **truncated** cone that you held to your ear. He had seen telephones just like it in gangster movies.

Caesar chuckled. "Somebody must've stolen it out of a phone booth," he said. "Then he got the money out and dumped it here."

"But the lock isn't broken," Charlie pointed out. "Maybe he had to get rid of it in a hurry."

When he shook the telephone, there was a dull [**clatter**] of coins. Caesar scrambled back to the wall and got a screwdriver. By the time he returned, Charlie had broken into the money box with a piece of concrete. They spread a piece of tar paper on the ground, and in the cold, smoggy **dusk** shook out the coins. Some were **welded** together by corrosion; most of them, however, were in surprisingly good condition.

"I hardly ever saw any quarters like these," said Charlie. "They must be pretty old. I don't know how old the phone is, but it doesn't even have a dial."

They counted the money. There was nine dollars and seventy-five cents! They [**sorted**] through the coins, **squinting** at them in the dark. Nearly all the nickles had buffaloes and Indians on them, and the dimes bore a woman's head, not Mr. Roosevelt's.

EXERCISE 1

SELF-TEST: After reading the above selection, do the following. Look at the Master Words below. Underline the words that you think you know. Circle the words that you are less sure about. Draw a square around the words you don't recognize.

MASTER WORDS

clatter	**dusk**	**reservoir**	**sort**	**truncated**
corrode	**perspiration**	**snatch**	**squint**	**weld**

Read the selection on the preceding page again, this time paying special attention to the ten Master Words. In the (a) spaces provided below, write down what you think is the meaning of the word. After you have attempted a definition for each word, look up the word in a dictionary. In the (b) spaces, copy the appropriate dictionary definition.

1. **clatter** (n.)

   a. ____

   b. a rattling noise, especially the sound made by hard objects knocking quickly together

2. **corrode** (v.)

   a. ____

   b. to eat away or wear away; to decay or rust

3. **dusk** (n.)

   a. ____

   b. a time between daylight and darkness in the evening

4. **perspiration** (n.)

   a. ____

   b. the moisture given off through the pores of the skin; sweat

5. **reservoir** (n.)

   a. ____

   b. the water supply for a large number of people; also, a place where anything is collected and stored

6. **snatch** (v.)

   a. ____

   b. to grasp or seize suddenly and quickly

7. **sort** (v.)

   a. ____

   b. to put in order or arrange according to kind or class; to classify

8. **squint** (v.)

   a. ____

   b. to look through partly closed eyes

9. **truncated** (adj.)

   a. ____

   b. cut off or shortened

10. **weld** (v.)

   a. ____

   b. to join metallic parts by heating, hammering, or both; to unite things so that they become one

Use the following list of synonyms and antonyms to fill in the blanks. Some words have no antonyms. In such cases, the antonym blanks have been marked with an X.

classify   extended   polish   rust   shortened   twilight
dawn   goggle   rattle   separate   silence   unite
disorganize   grab   release   sewer   sweat   waterworks
dryness   peer

	Synonyms	**Antonyms**
1. **perspiration**	(sweat)	(dryness)
2. **snatch**	(grab)	(release)
3. **reservoir**	(waterworks)	(sewer)
4. **corrode**	(rust)	(polish)
5. **truncated**	(shortened)	(extended)
6. **clatter**	(rattle)	(silence)
7. **dusk**	(twilight)	(dawn)
8. **weld**	(unite)	(separate)
9. **sort**	(classify)	(disorganize)
10. **squint**	(peer)	(goggle)

Decide whether the first pair in the items below are synonyms or antonyms. Then choose the Master Word that shows a similar relation to the word(s) preceding the blank.

1. wither	:flourish	::restore	: (corrode)
2. tumbler	:glass	::water supply	: (reservoir)
3. pluck	:snatch	::dampness	: (perspiration)
4. garret	:cellar	::sunrise	: (dusk)
5. grate	:fire holder	::reduced	: (truncated)
6. crisp	:soggy	::quiet	: (clatter)
7. flutter	:flurry	::organize	: (sort)
8. pomegranate	:seedy fruit	::peek	: (squint)
9. dart	:hobble	::drop	: (snatch)
10. appreciate	:insult	::detach	: (weld)

The Master Words in this lesson are repeated below. From the Master Words, choose the appropriate word for the blank in each of the following sentences. Write the word in the numbered space provided at the right.

clatter	dusk	reservoir	sort	truncated
corrode	perspiration	snatch	squint	weld

1. The saleswoman guaranteed that the metal on my car would not ...?... if I had it rust-proofed.

   1. ______ (corrode)

2. ...?... glistened on the shoulders of the basketball players as they stumbled toward the locker room after a tough game.

   2. ______ (Perspiration)

3. Lake Mead, the ...?... behind Hoover Dam, supplies water to most of Arizona, Nevada, and southern California.

   3. ______ (reservoir)

4. Many post offices employ machines that can "read" ZIP codes; thus, mail can be ...?...(d, ed) mechanically.

   4. ______ (sort)

5. In the cafeteria, the ...?... of dishes often interrupts conversation.

   5. ______ (clatter)

6. When we came out of the cave, we ...?...(d, ed) until our eyes adjusted to the bright sunlight.

   6. ______ (squint)

7. All the divers complained about the new, ...?... board, and they wanted the old, longer board back.

   7. ______ (truncated)

8. The Constitution ...?...(d, ed) the thirteen colonies into the United States of America.

   8. ______ (weld)

9. The squirrel ...?...(d, ed) up acorns to store away for winter.

   9. ______ (snatch)

10. You can begin looking for fireflies to appear after ...?... falls.

   10. ______ (dusk)

To complete this puzzle, fill in the Master Word associated with each phrase below. Then unscramble the circled letters to form a Master Word from Lesson 27, and define it.

1. often a sign of hard work — (p) e r s (p) i r a t i o n

2. pencils falling on the floor would do this — (c) l (a) t t e r

3. melt two pieces into one — w (e) l d

4. the trunk of a chopped tree is this — (t) r u n c a t e d

5. a shoplifter may do this — s n (a) t c h

6. stainless steel won't do this — c o (r) r o d e

7. what a bank teller does with money — s o r t

8. could be the site of a dam — r e s (e) r v o i r

9. vampire's wake-up time — d u s k

10. bright light may make you do this — s q u (i) n t

Unscrambled word: ______ (appreciate)

Definition: ______ (to realize the value, quality, or importance of)

(Note: Definition may vary.)

Read the following selection to get the general meaning. Read it a second time, paying special attention to the words in dark type. Notice how they are used in sentences. These are Master Words. These are the words you will be working with in this lesson.

From **The Red Pony**
by John Steinbeck

"That's old Easter," Jody explained. "That's the first horse my father ever had. He's thirty years old." He looked up into Gitano's old eyes for some **response**.

"No good any more," Gitano said.

Jody's father and Billy Buck came out of the barn and walked over.

"Too old to work," Gitano repeated. "Just eats and pretty soon dies."

Carl Tiflin caught the last words. He hated his **brutality** toward old Gitano, and so he became brutal again.

"It's a shame not to shoot Easter," he said. "It'd save him a lot of pains and rheumatism." He looked secretly at Gitano, to see whether he noticed the **parallel**, but the big bony hands did not move, nor did the dark eyes turn from the horse. "Old things ought to be put out of their **misery**," Jody's father went on. "One shot, a big noise, one big pain in the head maybe, and that's all. That's better than stiffness and sore teeth."

Billy Buck broke in. "They got a right to rest after they worked all of their life. Maybe they like to just walk around."

Carl had been looking **steadily** at the skinny horse. "You can't imagine now what Easter used to look like," he said softly. "High neck, deep chest, fine barrel. He could jump a five-bar gate in stride. I won a flat race on him when I was fifteen years old. I could of got two hundred dollars for him any time. You wouldn' think how pretty he was." He **checked** himself, for he hated softness. "But he ought to be shot now," he said.

"He's got a right to rest," Billy Buck insisted.

Jody's father had a **humorous** thought. He turned to Gitano. "If ham and eggs grew on a side-hill I'd turn you out to pasture too," he said. "But I can't **afford** to pasture you in my kitchen."

He laughed to Billy Buck about it as they went on toward the house. "Be a good thing for all of us if ham and eggs grew on the side-hills."

Jody knew how his father was **probing** for a place to hurt Gitano. He had been probed often. His father knew every place in the boy where a word would **fester**.

EXERCISE 1

SELF-TEST: After reading the above selection, do the following. Look at the Master Words below. Underline the words that you think you know. Circle the words that you are less sure about. Draw a square around the words you don't recognize.

MASTER WORDS

afford	**misery**
brutality	**parallel**
check	**probe**
fester	**response**
humorous	**steadily**

Read the selection on the preceding page again, this time paying special attention to the ten Master Words. In the (a) spaces provided below, write down what you think is the meaning of the word. After you have attempted a definition for each word, look up the word in a dictionary. In the (b) spaces, copy the appropriate dictionary definition.

1. **afford** (v.)

   a. _______________________________________

   b. to bear an expense; also, to spare

2. **brutality** (n.)

   a. _______________________________________

   b. the state of being savage, inhuman, or cruel; also, the state of being crude, coarse, or harsh

3. **check** (v.)

   a. _______________________________________

   b. to stop suddenly; to hold back or restrain

4. **fester** (v.)

   a. _______________________________________

   b. to become painful; to rankle

5. **humorous** (adj.)

   a. _______________________________________

   b. funny; comical; amusing

6. **misery** (n.)

   a. _______________________________________

   b. great suffering, pain, or unhappiness; wretchedness

7. **parallel** (n.)

   a. _______________________________________

   b. a similarity or resemblance; also a comparison

8. **probe** (v.)

   a. _______________________________________

   b. to examine thoroughly; to search; to investigate

9. **response** (n.)

   a. _______________________________________

   b. an answer or a reply; reaction

10. **steadily** (adv.)

    a. _______________________________________

    b. without wavering; without interruption; constantly

Use the following list of synonyms and antonyms to fill in the blanks. Some words have no antonyms. In such cases, the antonym blanks have been marked with an X.

bankrupt	constantly	funny	occasionally	reaction	soothe
bear	cover up	investigate	propel	serious	stimulus
bliss	cruelty	kindness	rankle	similarity	suffering
brake	difference				

	Synonyms	**Antonyms**
1. **response**	(reaction)	(stimulus)
2. **brutality**	(cruelty)	(kindness)
3. **parallel**	(similarity)	(difference)
4. **misery**	(suffering)	(bliss)
5. **steadily**	(constantly)	(occasionally)
6. **check**	(brake)	(propel)
7. **humorous**	(funny)	(serious)
8. **afford**	(bear)	(bankrupt)
9. **probe**	(investigate)	(cover up)
10. **fester**	(rankle)	(soothe)

Decide whether the first pair in the items below are synonyms or antonyms. Then choose the Master Word that shows a similar relation to the word(s) preceding the blank.

1. reservoir	:tank	::annoy	: (fester)
2. perspiration	:sweat	::search	: (probe)
3. corrode	:refinish	::gentleness	: (brutality)
4. truncated	:cropped	::support	: (afford)
5. dusk	:daybreak	::continue	: (check)
6. clatter	:stillness	::irregularly	: (steadily)
7. sort	:arrange	::reply	: (response)
8. squint	:peek	::resemblance	: (parallel)
9. snatch	:throw	::happiness	: (misery)
10. weld	:split	::grim	: (humorous)

The Master Words in this lesson are repeated below. From the Master Words, choose the appropriate word for the blank in each of the following sentences. Write the word in the numbered space provided at the right.

afford check humorous parallel response
brutality fester misery probe steadily

1. In ...?... to news of the flood, thousands of people sent clothing, food, and money to aid the victims.

2. The lawyer ...?...(d, ed) each testimony for possible lies.

3. Credit cards encourage many people to buy more than they can really ...?... .

4. The rain has fallen ...?... for three hours, so there is no doubt that the baseball game will be postponed.

5. The counselor told Lauren that she must express her anger and not allow bitterness to ...?... .

6. Bob drew (a, an) ...?... between the national debt and his own.

7. The police officer was charged with ...?... after doctors noted the thief's bruises.

8. From his pedestal the Happy Prince could see all the unhappiness and ...?... of wretched people in his city.

9. A situation or a joke is often ...?... because we are surprised by an unexpected turn of events.

10. The golfer ...?...(d, ed) her swing when she spotted someone directly ahead of her on the course.

1. _______ (response)

2. _______ (probe)

3. _______ (afford)

4. _______ (steadily)

5. _______ (fester)

6. _______ (parallel)

7. _______ (brutality)

8. _______ (misery)

9. _______ (humorous)

10. _______ (check)

To complete the crossword, choose the Master Word associated with each word or phrase below. Begin each answer in the square having the same number as the clue.

1. it's said to love company
2. to get information, you could do this
3. how to walk a tightrope
4. without money or time, you can't do this
5. a wound or anger might do this
6. what jokes are meant to be
7. inhuman treatment
8. hold back
9. an analogy
10. most questions deserve one

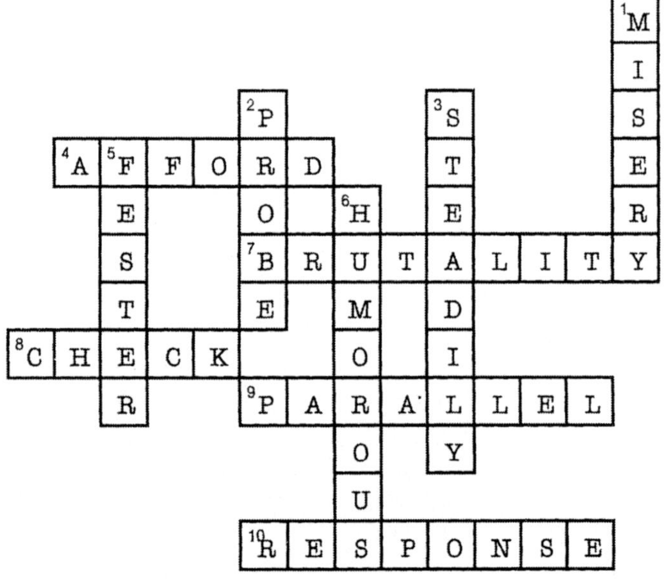

Read the following selection to get the general meaning. Read it a second time, paying special attention to the words in dark type. Notice how they are used in sentences. These are Master Words. These are the words you will be working with in this section.

from **Catherine, Called Birdy**
by Karen Cushman

I helped an ant today. She carried a **burden** so heavy it looked to crush her. A crumb it was, or a speck of wheat. Or a drop of honey that had hardened in the sun. She was struggling to take it back to her nest, where it would feed her **fellow** ants for a day or a week, as small as it was. So intent was she on carrying her crumb that she didn't notice me at all. I watched as she **staggered** and fell and bumped and stumbled, making slow **progress** toward what must have been her home.

But the day was nearly over. I knew the villagers would be driving their animals back through the **meadow** to pen them for the night. And the tiny ant and her **precious** crumb would be smashed into the dirt. I had to help her.

First I searched around for other ants, to see where they were going. I followed a line of ants running to and from a hole in the dirt, some in, some out, some sideways, all around the hole. This must be home, I thought.

I put a piece of a leaf in front of the ant. All intent on her burden and unaware of me, she walked onto the leaf. Then I went to the hole in the dirt where all the ant activity was. It was only a few steps for me but seemed a lifetime's journey for an ant. I put the leaf down by the hole. The ant walked around the leaf, up the stem and down the side, stumbled around in circles for a bit, **twitched** her **feelers** like my brother Robert **hitching** up his breeches, and walked down the ant hole, still balancing her **morsel**. I felt as though I had saved the whole world.

EXERCISE 1

SELF-TEST: After reading the above selection, do the following. Look at the Master Words below. Underline the words that you think you know. Circle the words that you are less sure about. Draw a square around the words you don't recognize.

MASTER WORDS

burden	**morsel**
feelers	**precious**
fellow	**progress**
hitching	**staggered**
meadow	**twitched**

Read the selection on the preceding page again, this time paying special attention to the ten Master Words. In the (a) spaces provided below, write down what you think is the meaning of the word. After you have attempted a definition for each word, look up the word in a dictionary. In the (b) spaces, copy the appropriate dictionary definition.

1. **burden** (n.)

   a. _______________________________

   b. ___load or responsibility___

2. **feelers** (n.)

   a. _______________________________

   b. ___antennae___

3. **fellow** (adj.)

   a. _______________________________

   b. ___peer; coworker___

4. **hitching** (v.)

   a. _______________________________

   b. ___moving by tugs___

5. **meadow** (n.)

   a. _______________________________

   b. ___grassy field___

6. **morsel** (n.)

   a. _______________________________

   b. ___small bit of food___

7. **precious** (adj.)

   a. _______________________________

   b. ___highly valuable___

8. **progress** (n.)

   a. _______________________________

   b. ___forward motion toward a goal___

9. **staggered** (v.)

   a. _______________________________

   b. ___stumbled or reeled from side to side___

10. **twitched** (v.)

   a. _______________________________

   b. ___jerked___

Use the following list of synonyms and antonyms to fill in the blanks. Some of the words have no antonyms. In such cases, the antonym blanks have been marked with an X.

antennae	load	releasing	tugging
floated	partner	smoothed	valuable
headway	pasture	stumbled	worthless
jerked	regression	tidbit	

	Synonyms	**Antonyms**
1. **burden**	(load)	X
2. **fellow**	(partner)	X
3. **staggered**	(stumbled)	X
4. **progress**	(headway)	(regression)
5. **meadow**	(pasture)	X
6. **precious**	(valuable)	(worthless)
7. **twitched**	(jerked)	(smoothed)
8. **feelers**	(antennae)	X
9. **hitching**	(tugging)	(releasing)
10. **morsel**	(tidbit)	X

Decide whether the first pair in the items below are synonyms or antonyms. Then choose the Master Word that shows a similar relation to the word(s) preceding the blank.

1. claws	:talons	::antennae	:	(feelers)
2. repulsive	:disgusting	::jerked	:	(twitched)
3. furtive	:sneaky	::pulling	:	(hitching)
4. complex	:simple	::cheap	:	(precious)
5. difficult	:arduous	::tidbit	:	(morsel)
6. nuance	:subtlety	::lurched	:	(staggered)
7. plummet	:drop	::grassy field	:	(meadow)
8. disoriented	:confused	::weight	:	(burden)
9. doubtful	:certain	::regression	:	(progress)
10. novice	:beginner	::peer	:	(fellow)

The Master Words in this lesson are repeated below. From the Master Words, choose the appropriate word for the blank in each of the following sentences. Write the word in the numbered space provided at the right.

burden	fellow	meadow	precious	staggered
feelers	hitching	morsel	progress	twitched

1. The wedding took place at dawn in a ...?... with spring wildflowers blooming as a bright carpet.

1. _______ (meadow) _______

2. She worked her way out of the crumpled car and ...?... back and forth to the side of the road.

2. _______ (staggered) _______

3. As he stared at the piece of cake on his plate, he declared. "I cannot eat another ...?... !"

3. _______ (morsel) _______

4. Whenever the exercises became painful, he thought of his slow but steady ...?... toward being able to walk again.

4. _______ (progress) _______

5. The robot used long sensors on the front to keep it from running into things, reminding her of an insect's ...?... .

5. _______ (feelers) _______

6. If she could save only one item, it would be her photo album, her most ...?... possession.

6. _______ (precious) _______

7. As though it were chasing a rabbit, the dog's legs ...?... in its sleep.

7. _______ (twitched) _______

8. The fifty-pound backpack was almost too much of a ...?... to bear.

8. _______ (burden) _______

9. The dress fit poorly, so she had to keep ...?... up the top to keep from tripping on the skirt.

9. _______ (hitching) _______

10. For the first time, Timothy felt the pride his ...?... teammates had been showing all season long.

10. _______ (fellow) _______

Use at least six of the Master Words in an original paragraph that tells or begins to tell a story. You may use different forms of the Master Words to suit your story.

Answers will vary. Here's an example:

The horse staggered along, pulling its burden of vegetables for market. Its progress was slow, and its ears twitched as the flies buzzed around them in the heat of the day. When they finally reached town and the horse was tied to the hitching post, all it could think about was the hope that some precious morsel of carrot or sugar cube might be its reward.

Read the following selection to get the general meaning. Read it a second time, paying special attention to the words in dark type. Notice how they are used in sentences. These are Master Words. These are the words you will be working with in this lesson.

From **Five Little Peppers and How They Grew** by Margaret Sidney

And then the carriage turned in at a brownstone gateway, and winding up among some fine old trees, stopped before a large, **stately residence** that in Polly's eye seemed like one of the castles of Ben's famous stories. And then Mr. King got out, and [proudly led] Polly out, and up the steps, while Jasper followed with Polly's bag, which he couldn't be **persuaded** to resign to Thomas. A stiff butler held the door open—and then, the rest was only a pleasant, confused **jumble** of kind welcoming words, smiling faces, with a background of high **spacious** walls, bright pictures, and soft, **elegant** hangings, everything and all **inextricably** mixed—till Polly herself seemed floating—away—away, fast to the Fairyland of her dreams. Now, Mr. King was handing her around, like a precious **parcel**, from one to the other—now Jasper was **bobbing** in and out everywhere, introducing her on all sides, and then Prince was jumping up and trying to lick her face every minute—but it was best of all when a lovely face looked down into hers and Jasper's sister bent to kiss her.

"I am *very* glad to have you here, little Polly." The words were simple, but Polly, lifting up her clear brown eyes, looked straight into the heart of the speaker, and from that moment never **ceased** to love her.

EXERCISE 1

SELF-TEST: After reading the above selection, do the following. Look at the Master Words below. Underline the words that you think you know. Circle the words that you are less sure about. Draw a square around the words you don't recognize.

MASTER WORDS

bob	**parcel**
cease	**persuade**
elegant	**residence**
inextricable	**spacious**
jumble	**stately**

Read the selection on the preceding page again, this time paying special attention to the ten Master Words. In the (a) spaces provided below, write down what you think is the meaning of the word. After you have attempted a definition for each word, look up the word in a dictionary. In the (b) spaces, copy the appropriate dictionary definition.

1. **bob** (v.)

   a. ____

   b. _____ to move up and down with short jerks _____

2. **cease** (v.)

   a. ____

   b. _____ to come to an end; to discontinue; to stop _____

3. **elegant** (adj.)

   a. ____

   b. _____ showing richness, refinement, and good taste _____

4. **inextricable** (adj.)

   a. ____

   b. _____ hopelessly tangled, complicated, or confused _____

5. **jumble** (n.)

   a. ____

   b. _____ a confused mixture; mess; disorder _____

6. **parcel** (n.)

   a. ____

   b. _____ a package or bundle _____

7. **persuade** (v.)

   a. ____

   b. _____ to convince one to act or believe in a certain way _____

8. **residence** (n.)

   a. ____

   b. _____ the place where one lives; dwelling place; home, especially a large house _____

9. **spacious** (adj.)

   a. ____

   b. _____ having much space; roomy _____

10. **stately** (adj.)

    a. ____

    b. _____ having a grand or majestic appearance; dignified; magnificent _____

Use the following list of synonyms and antonyms to fill in the blanks. Some words have no antonyms. In such cases, the antonym blanks have been marked with an X.

arrangement	convince	discourage	glide	lowly	refined
begin	cramped	disengaged	home	majestic	roomy
business	crude	entangled	jerk	package	stop
confusion					

	Synonyms	**Antonyms**
1. **stately**	(majestic) (refined)	(lowly) (crude)
2. **residence**	(home)	(business)
3. **persuade**	(convince)	(discourage)
4. **jumble**	(confusion)	(arrangement)
5. **spacious**	(roomy)	(cramped)
6. **elegant**	(refined) (majestic)	(crude) (lowly)
7. **inextricable**	(entangled)	(disengaged)
8. **parcel**	(package)	X
9. **bob**	(jerk)	(glide)
10. **cease**	(stop)	(begin)

Decide whether the first pair in the items below are synonyms or antonyms. Then choose the Master Word that shows a similar relation to the word(s) preceding the blank.

1. encounter	:face	::coax	: (persuade)
2. modest	:plain	::dwelling	: (residence)
3. retirement	:socializing	::humble	: (stately)
4. decent	:unfitting	::order	: (jumble)
5. sequestered	:secluded	::bundle	: (parcel)
6. rave	:mumble	::unrefined	: (elegant)
7. haunt	:hangout	::snarled	: (inextricable)
8. knoll	:rise	::big	: (spacious)
9. gloom	:sunniness	::slide	: (bob)
10. dell	:highland	::start	: (cease)

The Master Words in this lesson are repeated below. From the Master Words, choose the appropriate word for the blank in each of the following sentences. Write the word in the numbered space provided at the right.

| bob | elegant | jumble | persuade | spacious |
| cease | inextricable | parcel | residence | stately |

1. The strutting peacock, with his magnificent tail, is among the most ...?... members of the animal kingdom.

1. _______ (stately) (elegant)

2. As soon as the child realized that no one was going to pay attention to her fussing, she ...?...(d, ed) whining.

2. _______ (cease)

3. The pioneers eagerly awaited the Wells Fargo wagon for delivery of (a, an) ...?... .

3. _______ (parcel)

4. The maze Daedalus designed to house the Minotaur was so ...?... that the architect himself could not find his way out.

4. _______ (inextricable)

5. The Vatican is the official ...?... of the Pope.

5. _______ (residence)

6. The three boys gave their recitals of the adventure at the same time in (a, an) ...?... of excitement.

6. _______ (jumble)

7. Beginning swimmers are taught to ...?... in and out of the water in order to form the habit of rhythmic breathing.

7. _______ (bob)

8. Although Sally had many good suggestions, no one could ...?... her to run for student council president.

8. _______ (persuade)

9. The new station wagon seemed ...?... to the family after being crammed in a compact car for so many years.

9. _______ (spacious)

10. The house itself is modest, but the furnishings are ...?... .

10. _______ (elegant) (stately)

Order the words in each item from *least* to *most*. Use the abbreviations *L* for "least" and *M* for "most." Leave the line before the word of the middle degree blank. The first word provides a clue about how to arrange the words. See the example.

enthusiastic: _____inspired __L_hopeful __M_aggressive
(*Hopeful* indicates the least enthusiastic; *aggressive* indicates the most enthusiastic.)

1. roomy: _____enormous _(M)_infinite _(L)_spacious

2. sorted: _____assortment _(M)_organization _(L)_jumble

3. influencing: _____persuade _(L)_advise _(M)_brainwash

4. luxurious: _____tasteful _(L)_plain _(M)_elegant

5. bulky: _____letter _(L)_postcard _(M)_parcel

6. trapped: _(M)_inextricable _____troublesome _(L)_escapable

7. smooth: _____bob _(M)_skate _(L)_tumble

8. permanent: _(M)_residence _____dorm _(L)_hotel

9. fancy: _(M)_stately _(L)_crude _____modest

10. active: _____slow _(M)_race _(L)_cease

(Note: In some cases, answers may vary.)

Read the following selection to get the general meaning. Read it a second time, paying special attention to the words in dark type. Notice how they are used in sentences. These are Master Words. These are the words you will be working with in this lesson.

From **The Old Man and the Sea**
by Ernest Hemingway

Sometimes someone would speak in a boat. But most of the boats were silent except for the dip of the oars. They spread apart after they were out of the mouth of the **harbor** and each one headed for the part of the ocean where he hoped to find fish. The old man knew he was going far out and he left the smell of the land behind and rowed out into the clean early morning smell of the ocean. He saw the **phosphorescence** of the Gulfweed in the water as he rowed over the part of the ocean that the fishermen called the great well because there was a sudden deep of seven hundred fathoms where all sorts of fish **congregated** because of the **swirl** the current made against the steep walls of the floor of the ocean. Here there were **concentrations** of shrimp and bait fish and sometimes schools of squid in the deepest holes and these rose close to the **surface** at night where all the wandering fish fed on them.

In the dark the old man could feel the morning coming and as he rowed he heard the **trembling** sound as flying fish left the water and the hissing that their stiff set wings made as they **soared** away in the darkness. He was very fond of flying fish as they were his **principal** friends on the ocean. He was sorry for the birds, especially the small **delicate** dark terns that were always flying and looking and almost never finding, and he thought, the birds have a harder life than we do except for the robber birds and the heavy strong ones. Why did they make birds so delicate and fine as those sea swallows when the ocean can be so cruel? She is kind and very beautiful. But she can be so cruel and it comes so suddenly and such birds that fly, dipping and hunting, with their small sad voices are made too delicately for the sea.

EXERCISE 1

SELF-TEST: After reading the above selection, do the following. Look at the Master Words below. Underline the words that you think you know. Circle the words that you are less sure about. Draw a square around the words you don't recognize.

MASTER WORDS

concentration	principal
congregate	soar
delicate	surface
harbor	swirl
phosphorescence	tremble

Read the selection on the preceding page again, this time paying special attention to the ten Master Words. In the (a) spaces provided below, write down what you think is the meaning of the word. After you have attempted a definition for each word, look up the word in a dictionary. In the (b) spaces, copy the appropriate dictionary definition.

1. **concentration** (n.)

    a. _______________________________________

    b. _____ state of being gathered around a common center

2. **congregate** (v.)

    a. _______________________________________

    b. _____ to assemble; to come together in a crowd or mass

3. **delicate** (adj.)

    a. _______________________________________

    b. _____ easily damaged or injured; fragile

4. **harbor** (n.)

    a. _______________________________________

    b. _____ part of a body of water near the shore that offers ships protection from wind and waves, hence, any refuge

5. **phosphorescence** (n.)

    a. _______________________________________

    b. _____ the giving off of light without heat; light generated from living organisms

6. **principal** (adj.)

    a. _______________________________________

    b. _____ highest in rank or importance; foremost; chief; main

7. **soar** (v.)

    a. _______________________________________

    b. _____ to fly upward; to rise or ascend

8. **surface** (n.)

    a. _______________________________________

    b. _____ the outside of a thing; the top of a body of water

9. **swirl** (n.)

    a. _______________________________________

    b. _____ a whirling or twisting motion

10. **tremble** (v.)

    a. _______________________________________

    b. _____ to shake, shiver, or quiver

Use the following list of synonyms and antonyms to fill in the blanks. Some words have no antonyms. In such cases, the antonym blanks have been marked with an X.

be still	exterior	hardy	least	rise	spread
chief	fragile	haven	mass	scatter	swoop
collect	glow	interior	open sea	shake	whirl
darkness					

	Synonyms	**Antonyms**
1. **harbor**	(haven)	(open sea)
2. **phosphorescence**	(glow)	(darkness)
3. **congregate**	(collect)	(scatter)
4. **swirl**	(whirl)	X
5. **concentration**	(mass)	(spread)
6. **surface**	(exterior)	(interior)
7. **tremble**	(shake)	(be still)
8. **soar**	(rise)	(swoop)
9. **principal**	(chief)	(least)
10. **delicate**	(fragile)	(hardy)

EXERCISE 4

Decide whether the first pair in the items below are synonyms or antonyms. Then choose the Master Word that shows a similar relation to the word(s) preceding the blank.

1. persuade	:convert	::top	: (surface)
2. residence	:house	::shimmer	: (phosphorescence)
3. parcel	:packet	::port	: (harbor)
4. stately	:grand	::collection	: (concentration)
5. inextricable	:freed	::dip	: (soar)
6. spacious	:sizable	::spinning	: (swirl)
7. jumble	:system	::sturdy	: (delicate)
8. elegant	:coarse	::minor	: (principal)
9. bob	:bounce	::quiver	: (tremble)
10. cease	:commence	::disband	: (congregate)

LESSON THIRTY-TWO

The Master Words in this lesson are repeated below. From the Master Words, choose the appropriate word for the blank in each of the following sentences. Write the word in the numbered space provided at the right.

concentration	delicate	phosphorescence	soar	swirl
congregate	harbor	principal	surface	tremble

1. After we sanded and refinished the desk, its ...?... shone like new.

2. Hundreds of ants ...?...(d, ed) around the few drops of lemonade that had been spilled on the patio.

3. Max put away the ...?... glassware and got out the plastic tumblers when his little grandson came to visit.

4. A tiny ...?... of smoke in the distance indicated to the forest rangers that they had a fire to fight.

5. The ...?... was a welcome sight to the Pilgrims who had crossed the Atlantic on the *Mayflower*.

6. The hot air balloon ...?...(d, ed) over the city.

7. Does ...?... cause the fireflies to glow in the dark?

8. Steve's voice ...?...(d, ed) as he told about his narrow escape from the grizzly bear.

9. The automobile is the ...?... means of private transportation in the United States.

10. Texas has a considerable ...?... of people in Dallas and Houston.

1. _______ (surface)

2. _______ (congregate)

3. _______ (delicate)

4. _______ (swirl)

5. _______ (harbor)

6. _______ (soar)

7. _______ (phosphorescence)

8. _______ (tremble)

9. _______ (principal)

10. _______ (concentration)

Write the Master Word that is associated with each word group below. Then list three things that might be associated with the review word that follows.

1. sandpaper, table top, soap suds _______ (surface)

2. cold, earthquake, fear _______ (tremble)

3. shore, sailors, safety _______ (harbor)

4. hurricane, whirlpool, cotton candy _______ (swirl)

5. porcelain, silk, snowflakes _______ (delicate)

6. eagle, balloon, jet _______ (soar)

7. ship's captain, president, leading actor _______ (principal)

8. neon, glowworm, fireflies _______ (phosphorescence)

9. mother lode, crowd, black hole _______ (concentration)

10. concert hall, sports stadium, church _______ (congregate)

Review word: elegant (Lesson 31)

_______ (wedding)   _______ (coronation)   _______ (prom)

(Note: Answers may vary.)

Read the following selection to get the general meaning. Read it a second time, paying special attention to the words in dark type. Notice how they are used in sentences. These are Master Words. These are the words you will be working with in this section.

from **Chapters: My Growth as a Writer**
by Lois Duncan

I was thirteen years old, and it had not been a good day.

To begin with, I had **botched** up my first-period math test. Then, at noon, I had **discovered** that my lunch ticket had run out, and I had forgotten to take money to buy another. My **combination** lock had stuck, so I hadn't been able to get my gym clothes out of my locker and had received another **demerit** in P.E.

After school I'd gone to the **orthodontist** to have my braces tightened and been told that I'd have to wear them for at least another year because my teeth weren't lining up **properly**. Tonight was Carol Johnson's slumber party, and I had not been invited; why, I didn't know—I had always thought Carol liked me.

All in all, I was in a rotten mood as I slammed into the house and dropped my books in a heap on the coffee table.

"Is that you, honey?" Mother called from the kitchen. "There's mail for you on the piano."

I wasn't surprised. I got more mail than most teenagers dreamed of getting, all large **manila** envelopes addressed in my own **handwriting**.

But this was something different.

It was a narrow, white envelope with the name and address of a magazine in the top left corner, and when I opened it two pieces of paper fell out. One was a letter, and the other a check for twenty-five dollars.

I stood there, staring at both of them, too **stunned** to move. Then, slowly, I lifted the letter and read it.

"Mother?" I said weakly. "Mother?" My voice did not carry to the kitchen. I drew in a deep breath and let it out in an **explosive** shout. "Mother! They want it! They've bought it! *Calling All Girls* has bought my story!"

It was the most incredible moment of my life.

EXERCISE 1

SELF-TEST: After reading the above selection, do the following. Look at the Master Words below. Underline the words that you think you know. Circle the words that you are less sure about. Draw a square around the words you don't recognize.

MASTER WORDS

botched	**handwriting**
combination	**manila**
demerit	**orthodontist**
discovered	**properly**
explosive	**stunned**

Read the selection on the preceding page again, this time paying special attention to the ten Master Words. In the (a) spaces provided below, write down what you think is the meaning of the word. After you have attempted a definition for each word, look up the word in a dictionary. In the (b) spaces, copy the appropriate dictionary definition.

1. **botched** (v.)

   a. _______________________________________

   b. ___ bungled; made a mess of ___________

2. **combination** (n.)

   a. _______________________________________

   b. ___ ordered sequence of letters or numbers ___

3. **demerit** (n.)

   a. _______________________________________

   b. ___ mark against someone ______________

4. **discovered** (v.)

   a. _______________________________________

   b. ___ found out _________________________

5. **explosive** (adj.)

   a. _______________________________________

   b. ___ bursting with excitement or violence ___

6. **handwriting** (n.)

   a. _______________________________________

   b. ___ words written by hand; script ______

7. **manila** (adj.)

   a. _______________________________________

   b. ___ made of Manila hemp; strong brown paper ___

8. **orthodontist** (n.)

   a. _______________________________________

   b. ___ doctor who realigns teeth ___________

9. **properly** (adv.)

   a. _______________________________________

   b. ___ completely; appropriately __________

10. **stunned** (adj.)

    a. ______________________________________

    b. ___ shocked; overcome by astonishment ___

Use the following list of synonyms and antonyms to fill in the blanks. Some of the words have no antonyms. In such cases, the antonym blanks have been marked with an X.

brown paper
bungled
bursting
calmed

commendation
correctly
dental specialist
forgot

found out
incorrectly
mark against

mixture
peaceful
script

separation
shocked

	Synonyms	**Antonyms**
1. **botched**	(bungled)	(fixed)
2. **discovered**	(found out)	(forgot)
3. **combination**	(mixture)	(separation)
4. **demerit**	(mark against)	(commendation)
5. **orthodontist**	(dental specialist)	X
6. **properly**	(correctly)	(incorrectly)
7. **manila**	(brown paper)	X
8. **handwriting**	(script)	X
9. **stunned**	(shocked)	(calmed)
10. **explosive**	(bursting)	(peaceful)

Decide whether the first pair in the items below are synonyms or antonyms. Then choose the Master Word that shows a similar relation to the word(s) preceding the blank.

1. hunt	:forage	::brown paper	:	(manila)
2. dangerous	:precarious	::dazed	:	(stunned)
3. tight	:compact	::dental specialist	:	(orthodontist)
4. accept	:reject	::separation	:	(combination)
5. sociable	:outgoing	::learned	:	(discovered)
6. humility	:arrogance	::inappropriately	:	(properly)
7. fertile	:sterile	::commendation	:	(demerit)
8. scorned	:scoffed	::messed up	:	(botched)
9. disorderly	:chaotic	::bursting	:	(explosive)
10. erratic	:predictable	::typing	:	(handwriting)

The Master Words in this lesson are repeated below. From the Master Words, choose the appropriate word for the blank in each of the following sentences. Write the word in the numbered space provided at the right.

| botched | demerit | explosive | manila | properly |
| combination | discovered | handwriting | orthodontist | stunned |

1. After researching for many years, scientists finally ...?... a cure for the common cold!

1. _______ (discovered) _______

2. After all her bragging, how could she ever explain that she had totally ...?... the job?

2. _______ (botched) _______

3. If Gail had followed the assignment ...?... she would have passed the class.

3. _______ (properly) _______

4. He had always wanted to be an ...?... , but the tough grind of dental school sometimes made him question his decision.

4. _______ (orthodontist) _______

5. The two bullies facing each other on the playground caused a(n) ...?... situation that could have burst into violence.

5. _______ (explosive) _______

6. Another ...?... for running in the corridor might be cause for detention hall.

6. _______ (demerit) _______

7. She practiced her letters and numbers to ensure that her ...?... was legible.

7. _______ (handwriting) _______

8. The documents arrived in a simple ...?... envelope, yet they were the most important he would ever see in his life.

8. _______ (manila) _______

9. Though the team lead by twenty points at the half, they were ...?... to see it disappear and to lose the game.

9. _______ (stunned) _______

10. They were glad the bank safe had a(n) ...?... time lock, since they were forever losing keys.

10. _______ (combination) _______

Fill in the chart below with the Master Word that fits each set of clues. Part of Speech refers to the way the word is used in this lesson. Use a dictionary when necessary.

Number of Syllables	Part of Speech	Other Clues	Master Word
3	Verb	The singer was ...?... when an agent heard her perform.	1. ____ (discovered) ____
1	Adjective	how you'd feel if you learned you'd won $1,000,000	2. ____ (stunned) ____
3	Noun	what you might get if you're caught talking in class again	3. ____ (demerit) ____
3	Noun	Some think you can judge a person by analyzing this.	4. ____ (handwriting) ____
4	Adjective	an ordered sequence of numbers or letters	5. ____ (combination) ____
3	Adjective	a kind of paper made from Philippine hemp	6. ____ (manila) ____
3	Adverb	Parents want us to behave ...?... in public.	7. ____ (properly) ____

Read the following selection to get the general meaning. Read it a second time, paying special attention to the words in dark type. Notice how they are used in sentences. These are Master Words. These are the words you will be working with in this lesson.

From **Walden**
by Henry David Thoreau

I did not read books the first summer; I hoed beans. Nay, I often did better than this. There were times when I could not afford to **sacrifice** the bloom of the present moment to any work, whether of the head or hands. I love a broad **margin** to my life. Sometimes, in a summer morning, having taken my accustomed bath, I sat in my sunny doorway from sunrise till noon, **rapt** in **reverie**, **amidst** the pines and hickories and sumacs, in **undisturbed** **solitude** and stillness, while the birds sang around or **flitted** noiseless through the house, until by the sun falling in at my west window, or the noise of some traveler's wagon on the distant highway, I was reminded of the **lapse** of time. I grew in those seasons like corn in the night, and they were far better than any work of the hands would have been. They were not time subtracted from my life, but so much over and above my usual **allowance.**

EXERCISE 1

SELF-TEST: After reading the above selection, do the following. Look at the Master Words below. Underline the words that you think you know. Circle the words that you are less sure about. Draw a square around the words you don't recognize.

MASTER WORDS

allowance	**rapt**
amidst	**reverie**
flit	**sacrifice**
lapse	**solitude**
margin	**undisturbed**

Read the selection on the preceding page again, this time paying special attention to the ten Master Words. In the (a) spaces provided below, write down what you think is the meaning of the word. After you have attempted a definition for each word, look up the word in a dictionary. In the (b) spaces, copy the appropriate dictionary definition.

1. **allowance** (n.)

    a. ____

    b. _____ regular portion or granted share _____

2. **amidst** (prep.)

    a. ____

    b. _____ in the middle of; among _____

3. **flit** (v.)

    a. ____

    b. _____ to flutter; to move lightly and quickly; to dart _____

4. **lapse** (n.)

    a. ____

    b. _____ a slipping or passing away, as of time _____

5. **margin** (n.)

    a. ____

    b. _____ a limit to what is possible or desirable _____

6. **rapt** (adj.)

    a. ____

    b. _____ completely absorbed or involved in _____

7. **reverie** (n.)

    a. ____

    b. _____ dreaminess; fanciful thoughts _____

8. **sacrifice** (v.)

    a. ____

    b. _____ to give up something desirable in order to gain something else _____

9. **solitude** (n.)

    a. ____

    b. _____ the state of being alone or apart from others _____

10. **undisturbed** (adj.)

    a. ____

    b. _____ without interference or interruption _____

Use the following list of synonyms and antonyms to fill in the blanks. Some words have no antonyms. In such cases, the antonym blanks have been marked with an X.

absorbed	companionship	disrupted	outside	portion	stagnation
aloneness	dart	forfeit	passage	reality	uninterested
among	daydream	gain	plod	scope	uninterrupted
boundlessness					

	Synonyms	**Antonyms**
1. **sacrifice**	(forfeit)	(gain)
2. **margin**	(scope)	(boundlessness)
3. **rapt**	(absorbed)	(uninterested)
4. **reverie**	(daydream)	(reality)
5. **amidst**	(among)	(outside)
6. **undisturbed**	(uninterrupted)	(disrupted)
7. **solitude**	(aloneness)	(companionship)
8. **flit**	(dart)	(plod)
9. **lapse**	(passage)	(stagnation)
10. **allowance**	(portion)	X

Decide whether the first pair in the items below are synonyms or antonyms. Then choose the Master Word that shows a similar relation to the word(s) preceding the blank.

1. lounge	:idle	::border	: (margin)
2. tend	:lean	::flutter	: (flit)
3. rival	:supportive	::socializing	: (solitude)
4. quarantine	:sequestering	::share	: (allowance)
5. import	:ship overseas	::troubled	: (undisturbed)
6. scrupulous	:reckless	::existence	: (reverie)
7. slough	:remove	::give up	: (sacrifice)
8. renovation	:decay	::outside	: (amidst)
9. establishment	:shop	::period	: (lapse)
10. imperceptible	:evident	::bored	: (rapt)

The Master Words in this lesson are repeated below. From the Master Words, choose the appropriate word for the blank in each of the following sentences. Write the word in the numbered space provided at the right.

allowance	flit	margin	reverie	solitude
amidst	lapse	rapt	sacrifice	undisturbed

1. A beehive is one thing that is best left ...?... .

1. ___ (undisturbed)

2. Although the salesman continued to ...?... from one customer to another, he never seemed to make a sale.

2. ___ (flit)

3. Franklin realized that taking a part-time job would force him to ...?... some of the time he spent with his girlfriend.

3. ___ (sacrifice)

4. Rip Van Winkle had no idea that (a, an) ...?... of twenty years had occurred while he slept.

4. ___ (lapse)

5. Lucy felt small and unimportant as she stood ...?... the towering California redwoods.

5. ___ (amidst)

6. Michael is a loner who prefers ...?... even to the company of good friends.

6. ___ (solitude)

7. The ...?... for food makes up twenty percent of their budget.

7. ___ (allowance)

8. Aunt Helen was so ...?... in reading her book that she did not hear the knock on the door or the ring of the telephone.

8. ___ (rapt)

9. Bonnie tried to limit her immediate goals and narrow the ...?... of her possibilities.

9. ___ (margin)

10. People who spend much of their time in a ...?... tend to be impractical or creative geniuses.

10. ___ (reverie)

The invented words below are formed from parts of different Master Words from this lesson. Create a definition and indicate the part of speech for each word. The first one is done for you.

sacrifilitude   *(n.) the act of sacrificing one's solitude*

allowerie   ([n.] a dream about a big raise in your allowance)

marginflit   ([v.] to dart from one extreme to another)

raptifice   ([n.] a sacrifice made for the sake of a dearly loved person, hobby, etc.)

Now invent your own words by combining parts of the Master Words. Create a definition for each, and indicate the word's part of speech. (You may reuse any of the word parts above in new combinations.)

1. ___   ___

2. ___   ___

(Note: Answers will vary.)

Other possibilities:

raptflit	(v.)	to become infatuated with one person after another
reverapt	(adj.)	characterized by intense daydreaming
solifice	(v.)	giving up one's peace and quiet

Read the following selection to get the general meaning. Read it a second time, paying special attention to the words in dark type. Notice how they are used in sentences. These are Master Words. These are the words you will be working with in this section.

from **¡Yo!**
by Julia Alvarez

Yo and I walked to the bus stop the next morning, Yo **yakking** away about what it was like for her family that first year in this country. I took a deep breath of that **frosty** air and let it out so I could see something of myself in this **alien** world of bare trees, gray sky, brick houses, side by side. Then I told Yo my little secret. I had pretended to my teachers and classmates to be part of the García family. I kept my eyes fixed on the ground as I spoke. I could have taken a test on all the cracks, doggie poo, and **graffiti** on our walk to the bus stop and gotten an A+ for sure.

When I finished **confessing**, I expected some kind of **judgment**.

Instead, Yolanda said, "How'd you get away with it?"

"What do you mean?"

"You have a different last name, for one thing."

"I don't mean I told them I was a García. I... I..." This was hard. "I just made believe I live in your house with my own father and a mother who's not the maid." I could feel that tingling in my **nostrils** that meant tears were coming.

"Ay, Sarita." Yo had stopped walking. Her face was full of **delight** as if I had made up this story to please her. "You are my little sister of **affection**, and that's all anybody has to know about it!"

Why is it that if you hope for something with all your heart, and it's granted, you suddenly have this empty feeling? Or maybe it was just that **relief** made me feel a hundred pounds lighter, floating on air. She slipped her hand into mine. A gloved hand in a gloved hand—even a human touch was different in this country.

EXERCISE 1

SELF-TEST: After reading the above selection, do the following. Look at the Master Words below. Underline the words that you think you know. Circle the words that you are less sure about. Draw a square around the words you don't recognize.

MASTER WORDS

affection	**graffiti**
alien	**judgment**
confessing	**nostrils**
delight	**relief**
frosty	**yakking**

Read the selection on the preceding page again, this time paying special attention to the ten Master Words. In the (a) spaces provided below, write down what you think is the meaning of the word. After you have attempted a definition for each word, look up the word in a dictionary. In the (b) spaces, copy the appropriate dictionary definition.

1. **affection** (n.)

    a. _______________________________________

    b. ___tender attachment; fondness_________

2. **alien** (adj.)

    a. _______________________________________

    b. ___foreign or unfamiliar_______________

3. **confessing** (v.)

    a. _______________________________________

    b. ___admitting wrongdoing or faults______

4. **delight** (n.)

    a. _______________________________________

    b. ___great pleasure______________________

5. **frosty** (adj.)

    a. _______________________________________

    b. ___full of ice crystals; briskly cold___

6. **graffiti** (n.)

    a. _______________________________________

    b. ___messages written on public surfaces__

7. **judgment** (n.)

    a. _______________________________________

    b. ___official opinion or decision_________

8. **nostrils** (n.)

    a. _______________________________________

    b. ___external chambers of the nose; nares__

9. **relief** (n.)

    a. _______________________________________

    b. ___release from or easing of a burden___

10. **yakking** (v.)

    a. _______________________________________

    b. ___talking persistently; chattering____

Use the following list of synonyms and antonyms to fill in the blanks. Some of the words have no antonyms. In such cases, the antonym blanks have been marked with an X.

admitting   denying   familiar   nares   silent
chattering   disgust   fondness   pleasure   strange
decision   dislike   icy   release   warm
defacement   distress

	Synonyms	**Antonyms**
1. **yakking**	(chattering)	(silent)
2. **frosty**	(icy)	(warm)
3. **graffiti**	(defacement)	X
4. **nostrils**	(nares)	X
5. **relief**	(release)	(distress)
6. **delight**	(pleasure)	(disgust or dislike)
7. **affection**	(fondness)	(dislike or disgust)
8. **confessing**	(admitting)	(denying)
9. **judgment**	(decision)	X
10. **alien**	(strange)	(familiar)

Decide whether the first pair in the items below are synonyms or antonyms. Then choose the Master Word that shows a similar relation to the word(s) preceding the blank.

1. effective	:pointless	::distress	: (relief)
2. elicit	:bring out	::joy	: (delight)
3. energetic	:fatigued	::deny	: (confess)
4. gimmick	:trick	::jabbering	: (yakking)
5. vertigo	:dizziness	::unfamiliar	: (alien)
6. palace	:shack	::warm	: (frosty)
7. playful	:jolly	::opinion	: (judgment)
8. virtuous	:wicked	::antipathy	: (affection)
9. dry	:arid	::nares	: (nostrils)
10. lacking	:meager	::defacement	: (graffiti)

LESSON THIRTY-FIVE

The Master Words in this lesson are repeated below. From the Master Words, choose the appropriate word for the blank in each of the following sentences. Write the word in the numbered space provided at the right.

affection	confessing	frosty	judgment	relief
alien	delight	graffiti	nostrils	yakking

1. After ...?... his mistake to his parents, he felt better and was able to sleep.

1. _______ (confessing) _______

2. The cooling rain brought much needed ...?... from the overwhelming heat.

2. _______ (relief) _______

3. One usually thought of ...?... as vandalism, but the drawings on the wall were really works of art.

3. _______ (graffiti) _______

4. Using his best ...?... , he decided to turn in the wallet he had found.

4. _______ (judgment) _______

5. "If you would just stop ...?... for a moment, I could explain why we can't go to the movies," Shamall yelled.

5. _______ (yakking) _______

6. Even a light touch of one's hand can be a genuine sign of ...?....

6. _______ (affection) _______

7. Nothing could have looked more ...?... to these people than the bustling crowds and towering skyline.

7. _______ (alien) _______

8. The blooming garden, a babbling stream, and the sunny sky filled him with ...?....

8. _______ (delight) _______

9. The ...?... mug of root beer brought back pleasant memories of her youth.

9. _______ (frosty) _______

10. An acrid sting of smoke filled his ...?... , making it difficult for him to breathe.

10. _______ (nostrils) _______

Anagrams: Choose three of the Master Words. Write one at the top of each blank column below. Underneath each Master Word, write all the words you can think of that are made up of letters found in the Master Word. See the example.

judgment			
judge			
jug			
tug			
dug			
met			
gut			
tend			
gent			
dent			
men			

(Answers will vary. See example.)

Part I: From the list below, choose the appropriate word for each sentence that follows. Use each word only once. There will be two words left over.

allowance	concentration	incident	persuade	tremendous
burden	embroidering	margin	reservoir	undisturbed
clatter	garment	parcel	surface	

1. When his speech was over, Carlos felt as though a ____(tremendous)____ weight had been lifted off of him.

2. The P.O.W.s were granted (a, an) ____(allowance)____ of one bar of chocolate and one jar of coffee a month.

3. Both cars went through the stop sign at full speed, resulting in an ugly ____(incident)____.

4. During the dry spell, the city's ____(reservoir)____ reached its lowest level in twenty years.

5. Joseph's ____(garment)____ was a beautiful mix of colors and fabrics.

6. ____(Concentration)____ of wealth among a few people tends to produce just two classes: the very rich and the very poor.

7. (A, An) ____(parcel)____ too large for the mailbox was left at the post office.

8. The old woman sat on her porch painstakingly ____(embroidering)____ flowers on her grandaughter's dress.

9. The ____(clatter)____ of coins in his bank made Ron hopeful that he had finally saved enough to buy the model airplane.

10. Police officers were unable to ____(persuade)____ the suspect to surrender because the woman believed it was a trap.

11. Her broken wrist and upcoming final exams added to the ____(burden)____ she already carried.

12. Todd desperately needed rest, so we let him sleep ____(undisturbed)____ on the couch.

Part II: Decide whether the first pair in the items below are synonyms or antonyms. Then choose a Master Word from Lessons 25–35 that shows a similar relation to the word(s) preceding the blank. Do not repeat a Master Word that appears in the first column.

1. unsteady :stable ::distress : ____(relief)____

2. check :stop ::foreign : ____(alien)____

3. delicate :brittle ::broken down : ____(decrepit)____

4. properly :correctly ::pleasure : ____(delight)____

5. precious :valuable ::heartlessness : ____(brutality)____

    LESSON THIRTY-SIX

Part III: From the list below, choose the appropriate word for each sentence that follows. Use each word only once. There will be two words left over.

afford	discreet	resigned	solitude	stature
combination	guise	sacrifice	spacious	stunned
criticize	probe	snatch	squint	

1. Bob _______(snatch)_______ (d, ed) the last sandwich before anyone else could grab it.

2. Many people who are quick to _______(criticize)_______ the establishment are slow in suggesting ways to improve it.

3. Scientists are beginning to _______(probe)_______ outer space to determine what kind of life may exist on other planets.

4. The _______(discreet)_______ burglar removed all evidence connecting him to the crime.

5. The farmers affirmed that their dry corn crop could not _______(afford)_______ another week without rain.

6. Because they had a large lead and felt they would win, the team was _______(stunned)_______ when they lost the game.

7. Though Barb offered the invitation under the _______(guise)_______ of friendship, Ian suspected she had other reasons for asking him to attend.

8. Some psychologists believe that Napoleon sought power in order to make up for his small _______(stature)_______.

9. With their team trailing 62–39 at the two-minute warning, most of the fans were _______(resigned)_______ to the fact that their team would lose.

10. Karen will _______(sacrifice)_______ her daily candy bar and send the money she saves to a fund for hungry children.

11. At first Cory enjoyed the _______(solitude)_______ of the big empty house, but he soon began to long for company.

12. The mixture of ammonia and chlorine bleach made for an almost deadly _______(combination)_______ of ingredients.

Part IV: Decide whether the first pair in the items below are synonyms or antonyms. Then choose a Master Word from Lessons 25–35 that shows a similar relation to the word(s) preceding the blank. Do not repeat a Master Word that appears in the first column.

1. modest   :gaudy   ::uncertainly   : _______(steadily)_______

2. explosive   :quiet   ::regress   : _______(progress)_______

3. merchant   :shopkeeper   ::major   : _______(principal)_______

4. combination :mixture   ::gather   : _______(congregate)_______

5. sort   :categorize   ::hop   : _______(flit)_______

Lesson 1

alter
awareness
concept
dignity
heritage
historian
manuscript
masterwork
promoting
taxes

Lesson 2

account
admonitions
calisthenics
disciplinarian
economy
prospect
ration
recipient
singular
while

Lesson 3

antiseptic
aside
constant
distribute
hesitate
mechanical
murmur
pouch
relish
sympathy

Lesson 4

attitude
deny
devour
fretful
greedily
intent
munch
refresh
venture
wriggle

Lesson 5

adventurous
affirm
disengage
employ
immovable
imprudent
ironical
oblige
obstacle
rely

Lesson 6

blotter
chuckle
coincidence
gambit
gaze
irritate
philosophy
reflective
shrug
suspect

Lesson 7

antics
assume
duplication
exclaim
expert
intersect
junction
marvel
pattern
posse

Lesson 8

applicant
crumple
despair
dutiful
entirely
maitre d'
mislead
prop
suspicion
tilt

Lesson 9

excavate
expectation
haze
hunch
irregular
lurch
multicolored
opalescent
tingle
tinkle

Lesson 10

aggressive
altruism
brutality
chimpanzees
compassion
embrace
intensely
interactions
nurturing
seldom

Lesson 11

accustomed
charge
collective
conscientious
glee
individual
peep
rapture
smother
swoop

Lesson 13

dampen
humble
indefinite
latter
personage
preserve
select
society
substantial
sympathetic

Lesson 14

abandon
depict
dunce
pert
portly
protrude
rubicund
serviceable
trifle
valet

Lesson 15

beseech
blustery
chuck
engaged
exhaustion
goad
injustice
lodge
pitiful
slash

Lesson 16

bogged
ford
instinct
merciless
mill
plunge
resistance
submerge
treacherous
wrangler

Lesson 17

cloak
councilor
gilded
impractical
mutter
pedestal
reputation
sapphire
sensible
severe

Lesson 18

chute
clench
descent
desperate
flail
glimpse
hurtle
reserve
scramble
yowl

Lesson 19

captivity
conjure
deliverer
devise
enchantment
genie
implore
plight
rebel
vow

Lesson 20

characterize
expression
loophole
manifest
meek
nobility
rankle
resentment
steadfast
vigor

Lesson 21

acknowledge
destiny
existence
frank
inhabit
ordain
recital
render
restore
single

Lesson 22

accommodating
crestfallen
dwindle
economy
frolic
regale
revelation
strict
tidy
trace

Lesson 23

ally
annoyance
countenance
customary
foresee
inevitable
squall
tempestuous
tranquillity
wager

Lesson 25

decrepit
discreet
drowse
flawless
flicker
fragile
guise
refined
shabby
stature

Lesson 26

criticize
discomfit
garment
indicate
merchant
painstaking
rascal
resigned
smirk
sneer

Lesson 27

aired
camphor
chemise
embroidering
fix
incident
instance
manage
tremendous

unsteady

Lesson 28

clatter
corrode
dusk
perspiration
reservoir
snatch
sort
squint
truncated
weld

Lesson 29

afford
brutality
check
fester
humorous
misery
parallel
probe
response
steadily

Lesson 30

burden
feelers
fellow
hitching
meadow
morsel
precious

progress
staggered
twitched

Lesson 31

bob
cease
elegant
inextricable
jumble
parcel
persuade
residence
spacious
stately

Lesson 32

concentration
congregate
delicate
harbor
phosphorescence
principal
soar
surface
swirl
tremble

Lesson 33

botched
combination
demerit
discovered
explosive

handwriting
manila
orthodontist
properly
stunned

Lesson 34

allowance
amidst
flit
lapse
margin
rapt
reverie
sacrifice
solitude
undisturbed

Lesson 35

affection
alien
confessing
delight
frosty
graffiti
judgment
nostrils
relief
yakking

Glossary

A

abandon *v.* to leave, especially completely and forever; to forsake [14]

accommodating *adj.* eager to please; agreeable; willing to help [22]

account *v.* explain one's conduct [2]

accustomed *adj.* customary; usual; habitual; familiar through use or repeated experience [11]

acknowledge *v.* to recognize and accept as a fact; to admit [21]

admonitions *n.* advice or warnings against faults [2]

adventurous *adj.* involving a risk; courageous [5]

affection *n.* tender attachment; fondness [35]

affirm *v.* to declare something to be true or factual [5]

afford *v.* to bear an expense; also, to spare [29]

aggressive *adj.* marked by forceful energy [10]

aired *v.* freshened by exposing to the air [27]

alien *adj.* foreign or unfamiliar [35]

allowance *n.* regular portion or granted share [34]

ally *n.* one who gives another aid or cooperation; a supportive friend or associate [23]

alter *v.* modify or adjust [1]

altruism *n.* philanthropy; unselfish action to benefit others [10]

amidst *prep.* in the middle of; among [34]

annoyance *n.* irritation or disturbance; nuisance [23]

antics *n.* humorous, strange, or fantastic gestures, positions, or tricks [7]

antiseptic *adj.* thoroughly clean [3]

applicant *n.* one who applies for or requests a job, help, etc.; a candidate [8]

aside *adv.* apart (from); except (for); excluding [3]

assume *v.* to take for granted; to suppose [7]

attitude *n.* posture; physical position of the body [4]

awareness *n.* profound knowledge or understanding [1]

B

beseech *v.* to beg, implore, appeal, or plead [15]

blotter *n.* paper used for absorbing excess ink [6]

blustery *adj.* roaring; violent, as a strong wind or an angry person, often making empty threats; boisterous [15]

bob *v.* to move up and down with short jerks [31]

bogged *v.* to be sunk, as in wet, spongy ground [16]

botched *v.* bungled; made a mess of [33]

brutality *n.* cruel or beastly behavior; also, the state of being crude, coarse, or harsh [10], [29]

burden *n.* load or responsibility [30]

C

calisthenics *n.* exercises [2]

camphor *n.* insect repellent made from the camphor tree [27]

captivity *n.* imprisonment; bondage; confinement [19]

cease *v.* to come to an end; to discontinue; to stop [31]

characterize *v.* to mark or distinguish; to indicate a particular quality [20]

charge *v.* to trust with a responsibility or duty; to place a load or burden upon [11]

check *v.* to stop suddenly; to hold back or restrain [29]

chemise *n.* undergarment [27]

"""

Glossary

chimpanzees *n.* small African apes [10]

chuck *n.* a light tap or pat, especially under the chin [15]

chuckle *v.* to laugh quietly to oneself, often with the feeling of satisfaction [6]

chute *n.* an umbrella-shaped device used to slow free fall from an airplane or to slow speeding vehicles (informal for "parachute") [18]

clatter *n.* a rattling noise, especially the sound made by hard objects knocking quickly together [28]

clench *v.* to close tightly; also, to grasp firmly [18]

cloak *n.* a loose outer garment, usually without sleeves; cape [17]

coincidence *n.* an unusual occurrence of two or more events at one time, apparently by chance [6]

collective *adj.* having to do with a group of individuals viewed as a whole; mass; sum [11]

combination *n.* ordered sequence of letters or numbers [33]

compassion *n.* pity; sympathetic desire to help others [10]

concentration *n.* state of being gathered around a common center [32]

concept *n.* abstract idea [1]

confessing *v.* admitting wrongdoing or faults [35]

congregate *v.* to assemble; to come together in a crowd or mass [32]

conjure *v.* to solemnly request, beg, or appeal to [19]

conscientious *adj.* controlled by one's conscience or one's sense of right; just; upright; careful [11]

constant *adj.* continuing without a break [3]

corrode *v.* to eat away or wear away; to decay or rust [28]

councilor *n.* a member of a group that makes laws, gives advice, or manages government [17]

countenance *n.* the expression on the face; appearance; also, the face itself [23]

crestfallen *adj.* dejected; depressed; downcast [22]

criticize *v.* to judge, especially unfavorably; to find fault with [26]

crumple *v.* to crush together into folds or wrinkles; to rumple [8]

customary *adj.* according to the accepted way of doing things; usual; habitual [23]

D

dampen *v.* to depress, discourage, or deaden; also, to moisten [13]

decrepit *adj.* broken down; worn out or weakened by old age [25]

delicate *adj.* easily damaged or injured; fragile [32]

delight *n.* great pleasure [35]

deliverer *n.* one who rescues or releases another from an unpleasant or dangerous situation; a liberator [19]

demerit *n.* mark against someone [33]

deny *v.* to declare that something is untrue [4]

depict *v.* to give a picture of, often by use of words; to portray; to describe [14]

descent *n.* downward motion [18]

despair *n.* complete loss of hope, faith, or confidence [8]

desperate *adj.* driven to or produced by hopelessness; reckless, rash, or frantic because of despair [18]

destiny *n.* the power or force said to determine the course of events [21]

devise *v.* to think out; to plan; to scheme [19]

devour *v.* to eat quickly and hungrily [4]

dignity *n.* honor; esteem [1]

disciplinarian *n.* one who enforces rules [2]

discomfit *v.* to throw into a state of confusion or embarrassment [26]

discovered *v.* found out [33]

discreet *adj.* showing good judgment in behavior and speech; prudent; cautious [25]

disengage *v.* to release or detach; to set free [5]

Glossary

distribute *v.* to divide among several or many; to deal out [3]
drowse *v.* to be half asleep [25]
dunce *n.* a dull-witted or stupid person [14]
duplication *n.* a thing identical to something else; a replica or copy [7]
dusk *n.* a time between daylight and darkness in the evening [28]
dutiful *adj.* having a sense of duty or obligation; obedient; respectful [8]
dwindle *v.* to become less; to fade or waste away [22]

E

economy *n.* careful management of money, materials, or resources so as to avoid waste [2], [22]
elegant *adj.* showing richness, refinement, and good taste [31]
embrace *v.* touch with affection; hug [10]
embroidering *v.* decorating with needlework [27]
employ *v.* to make use of [5]
enchantment *n.* a magical spell or charm [19]
engaged *adj.* busy; occupied; involved [15]
entirely *adv.* wholly; fully; in all respects [8]
excavate *v.* to hollow out; to dig out [9]
exclaim *v.* to cry out or speak loudly, as from surprise or strong emotion [7]
exhaustion *n.* extreme weakness, fatigue, or weariness [15]
existence *n.* the manner of living; also, the state of being alive [21]
expectation *n.* an eager anticipation of an event [9]
expert *adj.* having special skill, knowledge, or training [7]
explosive *adj.* bursting with excitement or violence [33]
expression *n.* a look on the face that reveals one's feelings [20]

F

feelers *n.* antennae [30]
fellow *adj.* peer; coworker [30]
fester *v.* to become painful; to rankle [29]
fix *v.* direct one's attention; focus [27]
flail *v.* to throw one's arms or legs about wildly [18]
flawless *adj.* without any imperfection; faultless; perfect [25]
flicker *v.* to shine with a wavering light; to burn unsteadily [25]
flit *v.* to flutter; to move lightly and quickly; to dart [34]
ford *n.* a place where a body of water may be crossed by wading [16]
foresee *v.* to know or see beforehand; to have a vision of a future event [23]
fragile *adj.* easily broken; brittle; frail [25]
frank *adj.* truthful and open in speech; outspoken; candid; sincere [21]
fretful *adj.* irritable; worried; discontented; impatient [4]
frolic *n.* merrymaking; fun; carefree time [22]
frosty *adj.*-full of ice crystals; briskly cold [35]

G

gambit *n.* a maneuver by which one intends to gain an advantage over an opponent [6]
garment *n.* any article of clothing [26]
gaze *v.* to look at steadily or intently [6]
genie *n.* a spirit of Moslem mythology that works magic (also spelled jinni) [19]

Glossary

gilded *adj.* coated with a thin layer of gold [17]
glee *n.* joy; merriment; exultation; delight [11]
glimpse *n.* a hurried view [18]
goad *v.* to spur or urge on; to stimulate [15]
graffiti *n.* messages written on public surfaces [35]
greedily *adv.* eagerly; ravenously [4]
guise *n.* outward appearance, often with the purpose of deceiving or masking [25]

H

handwriting *n.* words written by hand; script [33]
harbor *n.* part of a body of water near the shore that offers ships protection from wind and waves, hence, any refuge [32]
haze *n.* a clouded mental state; a slight fog, mist, or smoke in the air [9]
heritage *n.* legacy; inherited possessions or traditions [1]
hesitate *v.* to pause briefly, perhaps due to doubt or indecision [3]
historian *n.* student or writer of history [1]
hitching *v.* moving by tugs [30]
humble *adj.* without pride or vanity; modest; meek; lowly [13]
humorous *adj.* funny; comical; amusing [29]
hunch *n.* a strong feeling, often not based on facts, that something will happen [9]
hurtle *v.* to move with great speed [18]

I

immovable *adj.* incapable of being moved; fixed; stationary; motionless [5]
implore *v.* to call upon, as for help; to beseech; to entreat; to beg [19]
impractical *adj.* unrealistic or idealistic [17]
imprudent *adj.* lacking caution and good judgment; rash; unwise [5]
incident *n.* minor occurrence dependent on something else [27]
indefinite *adj.* not clearly defined or with no set limits [13]
indicate *v.* to make known; to show; also, to point out [26]
individual *adj.* involving or concerning a single person or thing; particular; separate [11]
inevitable *adj.* impossible to avoid or escape; certain to happen [23]
inextricable adj. hopelessly tangled, complicated, or confused [31]
inhabit *v.* to live in; to make one's home in [21]
injustice *n.* unjust or unfair treatment or deed; wrong [15]
instance *n.* example [27]
instinct *n.* a natural impulse, especially in animals, which leads them to act without conscious thought; unlearned behavior [16]
intent *adj.* directed with eager or fixed attention [4]
intensely *adv.* extremely [10]
interactions *n.* mutual actions or influence [10]
intersect *v.* to meet or join by passing through or across [7]
ironical *adj.* mocking or sarcastic; implying the opposite of what is said or written [5]
irregular *adj.* not conforming to an expected pattern; lacking evenness and balance [9]
irritate *v.* to cause one to be impatient, angry, or displeased; to bother or annoy [6]

Glossary

J

judgment *n.* official opinion or decision [35]
jumble *n.* a confused mixture; mess; disorder [31]
junction *n.* a place where things, such as railroads, streets, or rivers, come together [7]

L

lapse *n.* a slipping or passing away, as of time [34]
latter *adj.* being the second of two things mentioned [13]
lodge *v.* to place firmly in a particular position; to embed [15]
loophole *n.* a small opening that offers a means of defense or escape [20]
lurch *v.* to roll or sway suddenly [9]

M

maitre d' *n.* the headwaiter in a restaurant [8]
manage *v.* handle or control [27]
manifest *v.* to make evident or obvious; to reveal; to show [20]
manila *adj.* made of Manila hemp; strong brown paper [33]
manuscript *n.* original, typed, or handwritten text [1]
margin *n.* a limit to what is possible or desirable [34]
marvel *n.* something that causes wonder or amazement [7]
masterwork *n.* masterpiece; supreme achievement [1]
meadow *n.* grassy field [30]
mechanical *adj.* performed as if by a machine or from habit [3]
meek *adj.* mild-tempered; patient; gentle [20]
merchant *n.* one who buys and sells goods for profit; a storekeeper or shopkeeper [26]
merciless *adj.* lacking compassion or forgiveness; cruel; harsh [16]
mill *v.* to move around in a confused or disorderly way [16]
misery *n.* great suffering, pain, or unhappiness; wretchedness [29]
mislead *v.* to lead into error of conduct or thought; to lead astray [8]
morsel *n.* small bit of food [30]
multicolored *adj.* consisting of many colors [9]
munch *v.* to chew steadily or vigorously, often with a crunching sound [4]
murmur *v.* to make a low, indistinct sound [3]
mutter *v.* to speak unclearly or in a low tone, often complaining [17]

N

nobility *n.* quality of being worthy or high in rank, mind, or character [20]
nostrils *n.* external chambers of the nose; nares [35]
nurturing *adj.* nourishing; training [10]

O

oblige *v.* to force as a result of circumstances; to bind or obligate [5]
obstacle *n.* that which stands in the way; a barrier [5]
opalescent *adj.* like a rainbow; reflecting an iridescent light [9]
ordain *v.* to establish by law, decree, or destiny [21]
orthodontist *n.* doctor who realigns teeth [33]

Glossary

P

painstaking *adj.* involving great care and concentration [26]
parallel *n.* a similarity or resemblance; also a comparison [29]
parcel *n.* a package or bundle [31]
pattern *n.* a design or arrangement; also, a model or guide [7]
pedestal *n.* a base or support, especially of a statue or pillar [17]
peep *v.* to look at slyly or secretly, especially through a small opening [11]
personage *n.* a person, especially one who is important or noteworthy [13]
perspiration *n.* the moisture given off through the pores of the skin; sweat [28]
persuade *v.* to convince one to act or believe in a certain way [31]
pert *adj.* bold; forward; lively; sassy [14]
philosophy *n.* a system of principles for guidance in daily living [6]
phosphorescence *n.* the giving off of light without heat; light generated from living organisms
pitiful *adj.* deserving of compassion, sympathy, or pity [15]
plight *n.* a state or situation, usually bad [19]
plunge *v.* to dive or thrust forcibly or suddenly, especially into a liquid [16]
portly *adj.* large in body; stout [14]
posse *n.* a group of persons with legal power to help a sheriff keep the peace [7]
pouch *n.* a bag or a sack [3]
precious *adj.* highly valuable [30]
preserve *v.* to keep safe from injury, destruction, or decay [13]
principal *adj.* highest in rank or importance; foremost; chief; main [32]
probe *v.* to examine thoroughly; to search; to investigate [29]
progress *n.* forward motion toward a goal [30]
promoting *v.* calling attention to; advertising or publicizing [1]
prop *v.* to prevent something from falling by placing something under or against it; also, to rest upon such a support [8]
properly *adv.* completely; appropriately [33]
prospect *n.* expectation; the mental picture of something to come [2]
protrude *v.* to stick out; to project [14]

R

rankle *v.* to keep within the mind irritation or resentment that becomes increasingly painful [20]
rapt *adj.* completely absorbed or involved in [34]
rapture *n.* extreme joy or delight; ecstasy [11]
rascal *n.* a mischievous or dishonest person [26]
ration *n.* a share or allowance as determined by supply [2]
rebel *v.* to resist or oppose authority [19]
recipient *n.* one who receives [2]
recital *n.* the act of telling a story, usually to an audience [21]
refined *adj.* free from crudeness or vulgarity; cultured; polished [25]
reflective *adj.* thoughtful; pondering; meditative [6]
refresh *v.* to restore strength or spirit to; to revive or put new life into [4]
regale *v.* to delight or entertain with something amusing, interesting, or pleasing [22]
relief *n.* release from or easing of a burden [35]
relish *v.* to take pleasure in, especially to eat or drink with pleasure [3]
rely, *v.* to count on; to depend on; to trust [5]
render *v.* to cause to be or become; to make [21]

reputation *n.* the opinion held of a person by others, sometimes different from the person's real character [17]

resentment *n.* anger or displeasure due to an injury or insult [20]

reserve *adj.* extra, as something kept back or saved [18]

reservoir *n.* the water supply for a large number of people; also, a place where anything is collected and stored [28]

residence *n.* the place where one lives; dwelling place; home, especially a large house [31]

resigned *adj.* showing patient acceptance of a bad, tiring, etc., situation; accepting; meek [26]

resistance *n.* a force that opposes or slows down a body or another force [16]

response *n.* an answer or a reply; reaction [29]

restore *v.* to return to an earlier condition; to renew [21]

revelation *n.* something that is disclosed to one who previously had no knowledge of it [22]

reverie *n.* dreaminess; fanciful thoughts [34]

rubicund *adj.* reddish or ruddy in complexion [14]

S

sacrifice *v.* to give up something desirable in order to gain something else [34]

sapphire *n.* a precious gem deep blue in color [17]

scramble *v.* to hurriedly and often clumsily struggle to get something [18]

seldom *adv.* rarely [10]

select *adj.* of special value or excellence; choice [13]

sensible *adj.* having common sense or good judgment; intelligent; reasonable [17]

serviceable *adj.* fit for performing a duty; useful [14]

severe *adj.* strict; stern; harsh [17]

shabby *adj.* appearing worn out; faded or ragged [25]

shrug *v.* to raise and lower the shoulders, often expressing uncertainty or indifference [6]

single *v.* (usually used with "out") to select from among a group; to set apart [21]

singular *adj.* exceptional; out of the ordinary [2]

slash *n.* a sweeping cutting motion [15]

smirk *n.* a self-satisfied or gloating smile [26]

smother *v.* to hide by covering up; to surpress; to suffocate [11]

snatch *v.* to grasp or seize suddenly and quickly [28]

sneer *v.* to express scorn or contempt [26]

soar *v.* to fly upward; to rise or ascend [32]

society *n.* a group of persons linked for any reason having common traditions and interests or ends [13]

solitude *n.* the state of being alone or apart from others [34]

sort *v.* to put in order or arrange according to kind or class; to classify [28]

spacious *adj.* having much space; roomy [31]

squall *n.* a gust of wind, often accompanied by rain, snow, or sleet [23]

squint *v.* to look through partly closed eyes [28]

staggered *v.* stumbled or reeled from side to side [30]

stately *adj.* having a grand or majestic appearance; dignified; magnificent [31]

stature *n.* height of a person or animal [25]

steadfast *adj.* faithful; loyal; true; fixed or unchanging [20]

steadily *adv.* without wavering; without interruption; constantly [29]

strict *adj.* governed by closely enforced rules; kept within narrow limits [22]

stunned *v.* shocked; overcome by astonishment [33]

submerge *v.* to cover, as by water [16]

Glossary

substantial *adj.* having body; solid; strong; firm [13]
surface *n.* the outside of a thing; the top of a body of water [32]
suspect *v.* to imagine something to be true or likely [6]
suspicion *n.* the feeling that something is wrong; uneasiness; distrust [8]
swirl *n.* a whirling or twisting motion [32]
swoop *v.* to descend suddenly; often in an attack [11]
sympathetic *adj.* having feelings of compassion or understanding [13]
sympathy *n.* the act of entering into and sharing the feelings or another person, especially pity [3]

T

taxes *v.* burdens; makes demands on [1]
tempestuous *adj.* stormy; violent; blustery [23]
tidy *v.* to make neat or orderly [22]
tilt *v.* to cause to lean, incline, slope, or slant [8]
tingle *v.* to feel a stinging, prickling, or thrilling sensation [9]
tinkle *n.* a short, light ringing sound [9]
trace *n.* a sign or a mark, often of something no longer present [22]
tranquillity *n.* calmness; peacefulness; quietness [23]
treacherous *adj.* not dependable; not to be trusted; deceptive; unreliable [16]
tremble *v.* to shake, shiver, or quiver [32]
tremendous *adj.* unusually large; huge [27]
trifle *n.* a little bit; a matter of small importance or value [14]
truncated *adj.* cut off or shortened [28]
twitched *v.* jerked [30]

U

undisturbed *adj.* without interference or interruption [34]
unsteady *adj.* not stable; shaky [27]

V

valet *n.* a servant or attendant who takes care of clothing and grooming of an employer or customers [14]
venture *v.* to dare to say at the risk of criticism, argument, etc. [4]
vigor *n.* mental or physical strength or energy [20]
vow *v.* to promise solemnly [19]

W

wager *n.* a bet [23]
weld *v.* to join metallic parts by heating, hammering, or both; to unite things so that they become one [28]
while *v.* to pass pleasantly [2]
wrangler *n.* one who herds cows or horses [16]
wriggle *v.* to twist to and fro; to squirm [4]

Y

yakking *v.* talking persistently; chattering [35]
yowl *v.* to give a long, loud, mournful cry [18]